"Depression is deeply personal and intense ir
find difficult to comprehend. That's why
crucial if we are to educate and combat public stigma. *Back from the Brink* does just that."

—**Geoffrey Gallop, DPhil**, professor and director of the graduate school of Government at the University of Sydney and former Premier of Western Australia

"Depression and bipolar disorder are serious illnesses, but they can be safely and effectively treated. The incredible personal stories in Cowan's book show that people suffering from these illnesses are not alone, and that recovery is possible. The practical advice contained in this book will provide a path to recovery, as well as hope that a fulfilling life is within everyone's reach."

—**C. Edward Coffey, MD**, vice president of Henry Ford Health System; CEO of Behavioral Health Services; and Kathleen and Earl Ward Chair of Psychiatry, Henry Ford Hospital

"*Back from the Brink* is an extraordinary collection of interviews with famous and not-so-famous individuals who have lived through the experience of depression and bipolar disorder. It provides invaluable insights and practical advice. It also sends the message, 'You are not alone,' to anyone struggling with mental illness, and reminds families and friends how much a difference their support can make in the journey toward recovery."

—**Michael J. Fitzpatrick, MSW**, executive director at NAMI (National Alliance on Mental Illness)

"Too many books about depression and bipolar disorder share only one person's thoughts and journey in dealing with one of these disorders. But in *Back from the Brink*, Graeme Cowan provides insightful and heartfelt interviews with eight others who've made the journey and come out the better for it. Cowan's engaging interview style and thoughtful questions make it easy to take away inspiration and hope from the book. Friends, family, and anyone who's grappled with depression or bipolar disorder will appreciate the worth of Cowan's valuable contribution."

—**John M. Grohol, PsyD**, founder of psychcentral.com, the leading online mental health network, and coauthor of *Self-Help That Works*

"Powerful personal testimonies from those of us who have experienced mental health problems can inspire as well as shift public perceptions. As we know from anti-stigma work at Time to Change, personal disclosure can dissolve stereotypes and support recovery. This amazing book really puts people in the driving seat of their own recovery and is helpful, hopeful, and empowering."

—**Sue Baker**, director of Time to Change

BACK FROM THE BRINK

true stories & practical help
for overcoming depression
& bipolar disorder

GRAEME COWAN

New Harbinger Publications, Inc.

Publisher's Note

This publication is designed to provide accurate and authoritative information in regard to the subject matter covered. It is sold with the understanding that the publisher is not engaged in rendering psychological, financial, legal, or other professional services. If expert assistance or counseling is needed, the services of a competent professional should be sought.

Distributed in Canada by Raincoast Books

New Harbinger Publications, Inc.
5674 Shattuck Avenue
Oakland, CA 94609
www.newharbinger.com

Cover design by Amy Shoup
Text design by Michele Waters-Kermes
Acquired by Melissa Kirk
Edited by Jasmine Star

Library of Congress Cataloging-in-Publication Data on file

Printed in the United States of America

15 14 13

10 9 8 7 6 5 4 3 2 1 First printing

My Suicide Note—July 24, 2004

My dear family,

Afte 4 long years of battling this illness I just can't take it any more. I feel I have tried everything and just can't see anything but a depressed future.

I would like to thank everyone for the loving care you have all shown me. I couldn't ask for anything more. Please don't blame yourselves in any possible way for this as there is nothing possibly that you could have done

Love always

Graeme

PS. I just can't be a burden any longe

I understand the despair of depression. I also now know it can be a gift. This is a book of hope.

Kind regards,

Graeme

CONTENTS

FOREWORD

When I stroll along the sidewalks and through the parks and public places of any city or town where people live their lives, I can't help but think that at least one in four of us, at any given moment, are touched in some way by mental illness. When I go across the street in New York's West Village to buy a carton of milk, I notice the people with whom I'm standing in line to pay and wonder if they, like me, come from a family touched by mental illness, or if they themselves are living with a mental illness. Of course we all have our public faces, the faces we choose or are forced by circumstance to show to the world. For those living with mental illness, that public face can be a vital means of survival, because to reveal what they are struggling with would open them up to the fear and shame of stigma and discrimination and make their struggle worse than it already is.

Everyone has a story. For those of us whose stories have to do with mental illness, being able to talk freely about our challenges and triumphs is the first step toward healing and being able to lead open, productive, and fulfilling lives. All of us need love and connection, and all of us need work that gives us a positive feeling of self-worth. The challenge of our times is to embrace and include those one-in-fours who, because of self-stigma or stigma imposed from the outside, have been unable to seek treatment and recover. In our stories lies our salvation. Finding the courage to tell our stories will save lives.

Since cofounding the anti-stigma campaign Bring Change 2 Mind, I have seen the power of stories to reduce stigma and provide hope. The stories in this book are deeply inspiring and provide practical insights into how those living with depression or bipolar disorder can lead a fulfilling life.

—Glenn Close
New York City
September 2013

ACKNOWLEDGMENTS

THEY SAY THAT A JOURNEY OF a thousand miles starts with the first step. Mind you, if I'd known it was going to be a thousand miles, I might not have taken that first step, but I'm glad I did. I have many people to thank for making this book a reality. After the success of my two books in Australia, I thought it would be relatively straightforward to take the concept to the world. How wrong I was. Before I acknowledge the people who helped with this book, I'd like to thank those who helped save me in the first place: My parents, Alan and Judy Cowan, believed in me when I could see nothing but hopelessness, and supported me when I couldn't support myself. My children, Melissa and Adam, were my main motivation to keep trying when I doubted I would ever get well again, and Melissa was also a great help in editing the interviews. My friend Ted Doraisamy helped me decide to write my first book on one of our many long walks. I now know that writing that book was an essential part of my recovery. To Gavin Larkin (who passed away in 2011), the inspirational founder of R U OK? Day (discussed in chapter 10), thank you for allowing me to be part of creating something great. I miss you, mate.

Professor Gordon Parker from the Black Dog Institute was encouraging about my Australian book before a single word was written, and he was kind enough to contribute to the first chapter of this book. John Draper, project director from the National Suicide Prevention Lifeline (in the United States), heard me speak about my book in Australia and encouraged me to consider doing a US version. He introduced me to the Depression and Bipolar Support Alliance (DBSA), where Allen Doederlein and Cindy Specht immediately embraced the idea of working together to produce a book like this, written with firsthand advice to help overcome depression or bipolar disorder. DBSA does such important work, and I'm delighted that they will receive 20 percent of the royalties from this book.

In 2009, I first met Rita Rosenkranz, my literary agent. I don't think either of us realized how long it would take for this project to come to fruition, and I deeply appreciate her patience and faith. She helped me find a suitable publisher and improve the proposal. My support manager, Sonja Firth, was diligent in bringing the many edits of chapters together in the final product, and in keeping me organized in all of my other activities.

Many US publishers ruled this book out because I'm from Australia, and "there are too many books about depression." I am deeply grateful that Melissa Kirk, an acquisition editor from New Harbinger Publications, was close enough to the subject to realize that firsthand advice would be valued by those close to the brink. Sincere thanks to Jasmine Star, the book's copy editor, whose patient and diligent review and thoughtful suggestions made the book stronger. Julie Bennett, New Harbinger's director of sales and marketing, and her team were enthusiastic and resourceful in thinking about the best ways to promote the book.

There are many others, too numerous to mention, who provided suggestions, contacts, and ideas that helped strengthen the book.

This leaves the interviewees: Patrick Kennedy, Trisha Goddard, Alastair Campbell, Lora Inman, Bob Boorstin, Cliff Richey, Jennifer Hentz Moyer, and Greg Montgomery. This book couldn't exist without you. Your honesty, courage, and genuine desire to help those who are suffering are truly admirable. Despite considerable cultural progress, depression and bipolar remain primarily secret illnesses. It's one thing to admit that you've suffered, and quite another to discuss your experience, in detail, publicly and for posterity. I admire each of you immensely. It was an honor and a pleasure getting to know you.

Finally, immense gratitude to my new wife, Karen Canfell, who has been with me every step of the way over the last two years. You provided humor, encouragement, and ideas, along with your considerable intellect, to help bring my dream to fruition. I love you for it.

INTRODUCTION

I UNDERSTAND THE UTTER DESPAIR OF DEPRESSION. I also now know that depression can be a gift if you're open to the lessons it provides. I know this can be hard to believe when all you see and feel is blackness and a lack of hope, but please read on.

I am so grateful for the life I now lead. I have wonderful health, two amazing kids (Melissa and Adam), a soul mate in Karen Canfell, a close and supportive family, and great friends. I live beside the Australian bush and am fortunate to walk in nature most days. I also have a career that's incredibly meaningful and fulfilling to me. I feel blessed. This wasn't always the case.

On July 24, 2004, I attempted suicide for the fourth time after a five-year episode of depression. My psychiatrist described it as the worst episode he had ever treated. During that period, I also lost my job as joint managing director of a management consulting company, experienced the trauma of separation and then divorce from a twenty-year marriage, had to leave the family home, and no longer had regular contact with my children. I completely lost hope that I could ever recover.

I hadn't accepted my depression passively. I tried twenty-three different medications, underwent electroconvulsive (shock) therapy on twenty occasions, tried transcranial magnetic stimulation, engaged in cognitive behavioral therapy, and participated in many other conventional programs related to the treatment of clinical depression. I also pursued alternative treatments, such as acupuncture, kinesiology, and self-improvement courses.

Even though I had beaten four previous episodes of depression, this was different. The black thoughts, pitiful energy levels, and complete loss of confidence seemed terminal. My mind couldn't grasp information, and I feared my intelligence was lost forever.

Although my journey has been about overcoming depression, my interviews of thousands of people with bipolar disorder revealed that we share similar struggles, stigma, and feelings of despair. While I appreciate that different medications are more effective for treating depression versus bipolar disorder, the majority of other strategies for healing are equally successful for both conditions, as underscored by the results of my 4,064-person survey, summarized in chapter 11. This book is for those with either depression or bipolar disorder.

Back to my story. After my marriage broke down, I was fortunate that my parents offered to take me in. This was a godsend, as by that time I was incapable of looking after myself. I left Sydney and moved up to Forster, a small coastal town about three hours north.

I was so grateful to have my parents' unconditional support, and, quite frankly, I wouldn't have made it without them. They believed in me when I didn't believe in myself. The downside was that I was away from my children and only saw them every two to three weeks. I was also away from my friends. I'd always had a wide circle of friends, and it was amazing how many of them had drifted away. I isolated myself, for sure, but I also sensed that many people felt uneasy about reaching out to someone who was mentally ill. Apart from family members, the only friend who visited me when I was hospitalized was Ted Doraisamy. There has been great progress in awareness of illnesses like clinical depression, but many people still fear them, and this manifests in avoidance.

Looking back, it's hard to comprehend the level of my despair in Forster. I felt my life was over, and every single day for two years I dreamed of the imagined bliss that death would bring. I couldn't imagine ever working again, being in a relationship, or making any sort of contribution. Death seemed like the only answer. Even though I had overcome severe depression before, it didn't seem remotely possible that this would happen again. That profound loss of hope was with me for a long time. Every day I walked to a cliff-top lookout and thought, *Wouldn't it be easy?*

I was fortunate to have income protection insurance from my previous job, so I didn't need to find paid work; but too much idle time can be a curse, especially with depression, which typically leads to an overactive mind and an underactive body. I decided to seek out voluntary work, but it was hard to find something I enjoyed and that allowed me to work with people in my age group rather than retirees, who made up most of the local population. Not that I was great company—far from it.

So I decided to find something to study to keep my mind occupied. I checked out the local technical college and found a computer course I thought I'd try. I wasn't fascinated by computers; my decision was primarily motivated by wanting to fill my days, which seemed all too long. But in class, I found it almost impossible to concentrate because my mind was clouded by both depression and antidepressants. I just couldn't do it, and that compounded my feeling of worthlessness.

One day I decided it was all too much. I couldn't go on. This was different from my three previous suicide attempts, when the decision to kill myself had been relatively impulsive. This time I'd been considering it seriously for a couple of years and had thought through many of the possibilities. My parents had gone away for the day on a tour, making this my best opportunity to end it. In addition to feeling that I couldn't just exist anymore, I also didn't want to remain a burden any longer and thought my family would be better off without me. With hindsight, and having since spoken with hundreds of families who have lost someone to suicide, I know now how insane that thinking was, but at the time it seemed logical.

My parents arrived home that day to find me unconscious in their bathroom. They found my suicide note. My mother knew the pain I'd been in for more than four years and that I'd made a very deliberate decision to end my life. For a moment, she considered leaving me as I was and not seeking help. She had seen her once-successful son become hopeless and lifeless, but the overwhelming urge to save her child took over. She described it as one of the most heart-wrenching decisions she ever had to make. As a parent myself, I hope I'm never placed in that position. A Christian woman, my mother resolved to call the ambulance and let my future be in God's hands. She knew God would make the right decision. He did.

The next day at about 2:30 p.m. I regained consciousness. I opened my eyes to find myself surrounded by my family. My daughter was holding my hand on one side, and my son on the other. My siblings had driven up from Sydney and were around me. I remember feeling quite calm and surprised that I didn't feel sick. It was embarrassing having the family I loved around me, all of them knowing I'd attempted to take my life, but it was also good to see them.

I'd love to say that after that fourth suicide attempt I had an epiphany and everything was wonderful. Unfortunately, that wasn't the case. Nine months later I was back in the hospital for treatment of my depression—more drugs and more electroconvulsive therapy. After a nine-week stay, I emerged a little better, but not much.

FINDING MY PATH

I did eventually find my way out of the black hole, but it was a long and difficult path. My primary experience was one of hopelessness, but eventually I came to understand that pain is evolution telling us we need to do something different. When I was chronically depressed, I yearned for stories of people who had been through something similar and had come out on the other side. Facts and figures can only take you so far. What I needed was a glimpse of optimism that could only come from fellow travelers—people who had been where I was.

I didn't feel confident that the usual treatments for depression could save me. I felt a huge sense of unease when I heard so-called experts say the only "evidence-based" methods for treating major depression were antidepressants and psychological counseling. I had no doubt that both of these treatments could be helpful, but to say they formed the complete picture was absurd. I'd already tried those approaches, and they hadn't worked for me. I also had some major reservations about the research approach that sought to identify and treat a single cause for my depression. I sensed that a silver bullet that would ensure long-term recovery didn't exist.

I had an idea about a book of interviews of people who had been depressed or had bipolar disorder and then recovered and were transformed by the experience. I wanted to find out which treatments and approaches people had found genuinely helpful. The trouble was, I was too depressed to do anything about this idea. But as I began to recover, and with the encouragement of my good friend Ted, I decided to begin the project. I had three objectives for readers of the book:

- To know that they were not alone
- To provide hope of recovery through firsthand stories and advice
- To encourage them to take action based on those insights

I interviewed prominent and everyday Australians: Geoff Gallop, former premier (governor) of Western Australia; two Olympic swimming gold medalists, John Konrads and Petria Thomas; Margaret Olley, an icon of the Australian art world who has since passed away; Les Murray, one of Australia's most famous poets; and seven everyday citizens. In 2007 I released the Australian version of *Back from the Brink*. Through writing the book, I found a purpose in all those years of suffering. It was a crucial part of my recovery.

I did eventually recover from my depression, and I describe my path in more detail in chapter 10. But having told you enough of my story to create some context, I'd like to turn to an issue you're probably wondering about: whether you'll ever get better.

WILL YOU EVER GET BETTER?

I remember constantly wondering whether I'd ever get better, and I'm sure you wonder about this as well. Depression is an insidious illness that's physically exhausting and mentally disabling, and it strikes when you're least able to fight it. One of the people interviewed in this book, Cliff Richey, describes it as a coward and a bully: a coward because it confronts you when you're at your weakest, and a bully because it tells you you're worthless. Like most cowards and bullies, it also backs away when you start making little steps of progress.

In this book you'll read the stories of people who have been courageous enough to tell it like it is. You'll know that you are not alone, and that others have walked in your shoes. You'll also learn how they gradually pulled themselves out of the deep pit of despair. All of them found that a combination of strategies eventually led to well-being. And as you'll see, recovery from depression seldom proceeds in a continuously upward trajectory. For most people, it's a bumpy road.

You may feel that your depression is worse than other people's or that no one understands the depth of your darkness and agitation. I know I did. I urge you to listen to the voices and lessons in this book with an open mind. You owe it to yourself and to your loved ones. It's okay to be skeptical, but don't be cynical.

This book is structured in three parts:

- **Information on depression and various treatments.** Chapter 1 describes the different types of depression, offers a self-test for depression, and discusses the latest scientific evidence regarding the most effective treatments.

- **Firsthand interviews.** Chapters 2 through 9 contain inspiring interviews of both high-profile and everyday people who have overcome depression. I am in awe of these people, who have shared so honestly about some of their most vulnerable times, and I think you will be as well. Chapter 10 provides more details about my own story and how I beat depression.

- **Advice gleaned from 4,064 fellow travelers.** I've surveyed many people who live with mood disorders and asked them to rate the treatment strategies that worked best for them. The findings are covered in chapter 11, Depression Treatments That Work, which includes practical advice and, in some cases, unconventional steps that can help you take control of your recovery.

Albert Einstein said, "Nothing happens unless something is moved" (2011, 482). If some advice resonates, it's important to take action. As you read on, keep these three points in mind (I'll expand on them at the end of chapter 11):

- Think in one-week chunks, making specific plans for each day and being sure to include pleasant activities.

- Set moderate goals.

- Celebrate progress—and be gentle with yourself.

Above all, listen and evaluate, then act. This isn't an academic book. It's a guide from and for fellow travelers. Just as a good travel book can enhance a foreign experience, this book has brought me immense benefits as I've listened to the authentic voices and advice of others—people who have been through something similar to my own experience. I hope you find the book similarly beneficial.

One final note: In the course of making hundreds of presentations on depression, I've found that an incredibly important way to assist and influence those who are suffering is to build the knowledge and resilience of their trusted loved ones. This book can also serve as a guide for family members and friends, so you might consider asking your loved ones to read it as well.

CHAPTER 1

UNDERSTANDING DEPRESSION AND BIPOLAR DISORDER AND THEIR TREATMENTS

MANY EXCELLENT BOOKS AND OTHER RESOURCES are devoted to a thorough discussion of depression, its causes, and its treatments. Because the focus of this book is the experience of people who have found a path out of depression, I won't go into the background information in depth. Rather, this chapter will provide basic information that may be useful to you as a quick overview of the causes and treatments of depression and bipolar disorder.

The information in this chapter was prepared by Professor Gordon Parker, founder and former executive director of the Black Dog Institute in Sydney, Australia (www.blackdoginstitute.org.au), an organization devoted to the diagnosis, treatment, and prevention of mood disorders. (The institute's name comes from a centuries-old nickname for depression, "the black dog," popularized by Winston Churchill.) I chose information from the Black Dog Institute because, as far as I know, it's the only mood disorder institution in the world that combines research, clinical services, and professional training programs for primary physicians and psychologists with community programs and information services for the general public. I believe that this broad approach provides the Black Dog Institute with a unique ability to communicate the latest research and its implications in a way that everyone can understand.

DEPRESSION

Depression is a common experience. We've all felt sad about something: a friend giving us the cold shoulder, marital misunderstandings, or tussles with teenage children. Sometimes we feel down for no reason at all. However, depression is considered to be an illness when the mood state is severe, if the feelings last for two weeks or more, or if it interferes with the ability to function at home or at work. To detect a clinical depression, clinicians suggest looking for the following signs:

- Lowered self-esteem or sense of self-worth
- Changes in sleep patterns, such as insomnia or broken sleep
- Changes in appetite or weight
- Reduced ability to control emotions such as pessimism, anger, guilt, irritability, and anxiety
- Emotions that vary throughout the day: for example, feeling worse in the morning and better as the day progresses
- Reduced capacity to experience pleasure—being unable to enjoy what's happening in the present, not looking forward

to anything, and losing interest in hobbies and other enjoyable pursuits

- Reduced pain tolerance—being less able to tolerate aches and pains and possibly having a host of new ailments
- Reduced or nonexistent sex drive
- Poor concentration and memory—occasionally to the extent that people think they're demented
- Reduced motivation—a feeling of meaninglessness or that nothing is worth doing
- Lowered energy levels

Bear in mind that other diseases can produce these symptoms. This is one of the key reasons that you need to seek an accurate diagnosis from your general practitioner or another qualified health care professional.

Types of Depression

Various mental health organizations recognize different subtypes of depression. In Professor Parker's model, clinical depression can be categorized into three subtypes, each with its own features and causes: melancholic depression, nonmelancholic depression, and psychotic depression. There may be a fourth type: atypical depression. Knowing that there are different types of depression is important because each type responds best to different treatments.

Depression can also be subtyped into two categories, unipolar depression and bipolar disorder. In unipolar depression, only depressive episodes are experienced, whereas in bipolar disorder, people experience manic or hypomanic times as well as depressive episodes. Researchers at the Black Dog Institute have found that in bipolar disorder, depression is most likely to be of a melancholic or psychotic type (Parker et al. 2012).

MELANCHOLIC DEPRESSION

Melancholic depression is the classic form of biological depression. Its defining features are psychomotor disturbances, usually showing up as slowed or agitated physical movements and slowed thinking, combined with a more severe and nonresponsive mood state than seen in nonmelancholic depression.

Melancholic depression is a relatively uncommon type of depression. It affects approximately 10 percent of patients with mood disorders seeking primary care (Parker and Hadzi-Pavlovic 1996). The numbers of men and women affected are roughly the same.

This type of depression has a low spontaneous remission rate. It responds best to physical treatments, such as antidepressant drugs, and only minimally, at best, to nonphysical treatments, such as counseling or psychotherapy (Parker and Hadzi-Pavlovic 1996).

NONMELANCHOLIC DEPRESSION

Nonmelancholic depression is essentially depression that isn't melancholic—in other words, it isn't primarily biological. Instead, it has psychosocial causes and is often linked to stressful events in a person's life, sometimes in combination with the individual's personality. (The particular personality types that can contribute to depression are discussed later in this chapter.)

Nonmelancholic depression is the most common of the three types of depression. It can be hard to accurately diagnose because it lacks the defining characteristics of the other two types of depression: slowed or agitated physical movements and slowed thinking, or psychotic features. Also in contrast to the other two types of depression, people with nonmelancholic depression can usually be cheered up to some degree.

Nonmelancholic depression also has a higher rate of spontaneous remission than the other types of depression (Parker and Manicavasagar 2005). This is because it's often linked to stressful events in a person's life, and when the stress is resolved, the depression tends to lift. Nonmelancholic depression responds variably to a number of different types of treatment, such as psychotherapies, antidepressants, and counseling (Parker and Manicavasagar 2005). The treatment selected should be linked to the cause. For example, if the depression appears to be related to personality style, such as being an excessive worrier or perfectionistic, cognitive behavioral therapy might be a better choice; whereas if it's related to stress, counseling might be preferable.

PSYCHOTIC DEPRESSION

Psychotic depression is less common than either melancholic or nonmelancholic depression. The defining features of psychotic depression are a more severely depressed mood than is the case with either melancholic or nonmelancholic depression, more severe psychomotor disturbances than occur in melancholic depression, psychotic symptoms (delusions or, more rarely, hallucinations), and strong feelings of guilt. Psychotic depression is somewhat more likely than nonpsychotic depression in older people and in the postpartum period.

Psychotic depression has a low spontaneous remission rate. It responds best to physical treatments, such as antidepressant and antipsychotic drugs, and not to psychotherapy (Parker et al. 1991).

ATYPICAL DEPRESSION

Atypical depression is a diagnosis given to symptoms of depression that contrast with the usual characteristics of nonmelancholic depression. For example, the person experiences increased appetite rather than appetite loss, and sleepiness rather than insomnia. Another common symptom is arms and legs feeling heavy and leaden. People with atypical depression are also likely to have a personality style of interpersonal hypersensitivity, meaning they expect that others will reject or abandon them. However, as with nonmelancholic depression, people with atypical depression can often be cheered up by pleasant events.

BIPOLAR DISORDER

Bipolar disorder is the name used to describe a set of conditions characterized by mood swings. The most severe form of bipolar disorder used to be called manic depression. In current terminology, bipolar I disorder is more severe, with people having longer periods of high mood, and being more likely to have psychotic symptoms and be hospitalized. In addition, people with bipolar I disorder experience true mania, whereas those with bipolar II disorder experience hypomania and are often fully functioning. Bipolar II disorder is generally viewed as less severe because it doesn't include psychotic symptoms, but studies suggest that impairment and thoughts of suicide are often as severe in bipolar II as in bipolar I disorder (Parker 2012).

Causes of Depression

In contrast to some illnesses and disorders, there is no simple explanation for what causes depression. Each type of depression is likely to have different mixtures of causes. In psychotic or melancholic depression, physical and biological factors are generally more relevant, whereas in nonmelancholic depression, personality and stressful life events are usually more relevant. Among the many potential causes are genetics, biochemical factors, aging of the brain, gender, stress, and personality.

GENETICS

Contrary to the popular view that depression is primarily caused by life experiences, personality, or a combination of those factors, strong evidence indicates that genetics are a significant factor in a person's predisposition toward developing melancholic or psychotic depression or bipolar disorder. The genetic risk of developing these two types is about 40 percent (Glowinski et al. 2003).

BIOCHEMICAL FACTORS

In most instances of clinical depression, it's likely that neurotransmitter function is disrupted, distinctly so for melancholic and psychotic depression. Neurotransmitters are chemicals that carry signals within the brain and throughout the nervous system. Many different neurotransmitters exist, serving different purposes; however, three are especially important in influencing mood: serotonin, norepinephrine, and dopamine.

In normal brain function, neurotransmitters travel from one nerve cell to the next, transmitting electrical impulses that remain as strong in the second and subsequent cells as in the first. In people who are depressed, mood-regulating neurotransmitters fail to function normally, and, as a result, the signal is disrupted or diminished.

AGING OF THE BRAIN

As we age, the brain's general functioning diminishes, and levels of certain neurotransmitters that influence mood state may also be affected. Elderly people who are developing dementia may at some point (often early on) develop severe depression for the first time. This depression is usually psychotic or melancholic and is a reflection of the disruption of circuits linking certain regions of the brain. Sometimes these changes are merely a reflection of the aging process, particularly in people who are vulnerable to this kind of wear and tear. In others, however, high blood pressure or mini-strokes, which are often unnoticed by the individual and family members, may contribute (Parker and Hadzi-Pavlovic 1996).

GENDER

Gender can play a role in some types of depression. Essentially equal numbers of men and women develop melancholic depression;

however, women are much more likely to develop nonmelancholic depression than men. There are a number of explanations for this.

Women are more likely than men to internalize stress, which places them at greater risk of developing depression. Additionally, women with unsatisfactory marriages or many young children are disproportionately likely to be depressed, suggesting that social stress is playing a role.

Hormonal influences that begin in puberty may account for women's increased likelihood of developing anxiety, which is a precursor to depression, or depression itself. However, although sex hormones or biological differences may create a greater likelihood that women will develop depression, certain social factors must come into play for depression to arise.

STRESS

It's important to recognize that everyone is subject to stress, and that this stress can lead to a low mood. Most people get over the stress or low mood within days or weeks, but others don't.

Past and long-standing stresses can increase the chance of developing depression in later years. An example is having an abusive or uncaring parent, which may result in the child developing low self-esteem and thus being vulnerable to depression in adult life.

Most people who develop nonmelancholic depression describe a significant life event that precipitated the depression. The events most likely to trigger depression are those that damage or compromise a person's self-esteem. For most adults, self-esteem is closely linked to intimate relationships and other important domains of life, such as work. The breakup of a marriage or other close relationship is a common trigger for depression. Other people develop depression because they feel a sense of shame, often due to believing they haven't lived up to their own or others' expectations, which results in lowered self-esteem.

PERSONALITY

Research at the Black Dog Institute has shown that people with particular personality types are more at risk of developing depression than others (Parker and Manicavasagar 2005). These include people with the following traits:

- High levels of anxiety, which may be experienced as internalized worrying or as a more externalized irritability
- Shyness, expressed as social avoidance, being reserved, or both
- Self-criticism or a low sense of self-worth
- High levels of interpersonal sensitivity

Those who prominently display features of these personality types are at greater risk of developing nonmelancholic depression.

SELF-TESTING FOR DEPRESSION

Below you'll find a self-test for clinical depression developed by Professor Parker. It also identifies possible symptoms of bipolar disorder. (The test is available at www.blackdoginstitute.org.au, where you can take the test online and get your score. The website also offers a self-test for bipolar disorder.)

Please note that while great care was taken with the development of this self-assessment tool, it isn't intended to be a substitute for professional advice. While the results of the self-test may be helpful, you should always seek the advice of a qualified health care practitioner with any questions you have regarding your health, mental or physical.

Please consider the following questions and rate how true each is in relation to how you've been feeling lately (in the last two to three days) compared to how you normally feel.

	Not true	Slightly true	Moderately true	Very true
Are you stewing over things?				
Do you feel more vulnerable than usual?				
Are you being more self-critical and hard on yourself?				
Are you feeling guilty about things in your life?				
Do you find that nothing seems to be able to cheer you up?				
Do you feel as if you have lost your core and essence?				
Are you feeling depressed?				
Do you feel less worthwhile?				
Do you feel hopeless or helpless?				
Do you feel more distant from other people?				

Scores can be obtained online at http://www.blackdoginstitute.org.au/public/depression/self-test.cfm.

TREATMENTS FOR DEPRESSION AND BIPOLAR DISORDER

Due to the significant amount of ongoing research on depression treatments, new approaches are constantly emerging, ranging from prescription medications to self-help and alternative medicine therapies. Continuing research means that the evidence for how well a given treatment works is also subject to change. The key to finding the treatment approach that's right for you is to get a sophisticated assessment. While a depressive episode may lift spontaneously over time, there's no guarantee that this will happen. With the treatments that are available today, no one needs to suffer unnecessarily or for a long period of time.

Researchers at the Black Dog Institute believe that treatments should be selected based on the type of depression a person has (Parker and Manicavasagar 2005). The types that are more biological in nature, melancholic and psychotic depression, are more likely to require physical treatments and less likely to be resolved with psychological treatments alone. On the other hand, psychological treatments are usually the first step in treating nonmelancholic depression; however, physical treatments, such as antidepressants, are sometimes used if symptoms are particularly persistent and significantly affect other areas of life.

Physical Treatments

The main physical treatments for depression are medications and electroconvulsive therapy, or shock therapy. A third physical treatment, which hasn't yet been widely applied, is transcranial magnetic stimulation.

MEDICATIONS

The three groups of drugs most likely to be used for depression are antidepressants, tranquilizers, and mood stabilizers, the latter also known as antimanic drugs. For people with bipolar depression, taking antidepressants alone can be dangerous because doing so may induce mania. This is one reason why it's essential to get an accurate diagnosis and work with a prescribing practitioner who has significant experience in successfully treating mood disorders.

Antidepressants. A wide variety of antidepressants are available, and they can help with many types of depression. Their effectiveness varies depending on the type of depression and other factors. Selective serotonin reuptake inhibitors (SSRIs), serotonin and norepinephrine reuptake inhibitors (SNRIs), tricyclics (TCAs), and monoamine oxidase inhibitors (MAOIs) are four common classes of antidepressants. SSRIs are narrow-action drugs that increase levels of the neurotransmitter serotonin in the brain by blocking their reabsorption. SNRIs are dual-action drugs that increase levels of both serotonin and norepinephrine in the same way. TCAs and MAOIs are broad-action drugs that exert wider effects, increasing levels of multiple neurotransmitters. For melancholic depression, the broader-action medications (preferably TCAs and MAOIs, but also SNRIs) are more effective, while for nonmelancholic depression, all classes of antidepressants seem to have comparable levels of effectiveness, though they are not always required. Many clinicians believe it's important to find the right antidepressant, as different antidepressants produce different effects and outcomes in people with different subtypes of depression.

Tranquilizers. Tranquilizers can be classified as minor or major. Minor tranquilizers (typically a class of drug called benzodiazepines) aren't helpful in depression. In fact, they're addictive and can make depression worse. Major tranquilizers, however, are quite useful in treating psychotic or melancholic depression where other medications haven't proven helpful. They're usually used to augment other treatments, and are discontinued once the depression has lifted (Parker and Manicavasagar 2005).

Mood stabilizers. Also known as antimanic drugs, mood stabilizers are of great importance in bipolar disorder. As their name indicates, they are useful for treating mania, and their ability to reduce the severity and frequency of mood swings helps them stabilize mood. Lithium, valproate (Depakote), lamotrigine (Lamictal), and carbamazepine (Tegretol) are the most common mood stabilizers.

A well-informed health professional should be able to identify the medication most likely to benefit any given individual based on assessment of the type of depression, its likely causes, and an understanding of the patient. A final note on medications: It's important to understand that antidepressants and mood stabilizers are often necessary both to treat any current depressive episode and to make a future relapse less likely. Consequently, people may need to continue taking these medications for some time after they're better.

ELECTROCONVULSIVE THERAPY

Because of its controversial past, many people feel cautious about having electroconvulsive therapy (ECT) or allowing this treatment to be used on loved ones. However, it has a small but important role when other drug treatments have failed, particularly in cases of psychotic depression, life-threatening mania, severe postpartum depression, or severe melancholic depression where there is a high risk of suicide or the patient is too ill to eat, drink, or take medications.

While ECT does have some short-term side effects, it's relatively safe, and because a general anesthetic is used, it isn't too unpleasant. A carefully controlled electrical current is passed between two electrodes placed on the scalp and travels through the brain, affecting the brain's electrical activity. On waking, the person has no memory of what occurred after administration of the anesthetic.

Immediately after treatment, the most common adverse effects are confusion and memory loss. The state of confusion usually disappears after a few hours, but the short-term memory loss can last longer.

TRANSCRANIAL MAGNETIC STIMULATION

A possible alternative to ECT is transcranial magnetic stimulation (TMS), a procedure used by neurologists as both a treatment and a diagnostic strategy. Using a coil held next to the patient's head, a magnetic field is created to stimulate certain parts of the brain. There is no need for a general anesthetic, and a convulsion isn't induced.

The evidence in favor of this treatment isn't definitive yet, but it is a major area of research. If TMS is shown to be as effective as ECT, this would be a distinct advance in the treatment of many mood disorders. Unfortunately, it will probably be several years before we have clear evidence about its utility.

Psychological Treatments

Many different psychological treatments are used for depression. Here are some of the most common:

- Cognitive behavioral therapy
- Interpersonal therapy
- Mindfulness-based cognitive therapy
- Acceptance and commitment therapy
- Psychoanalysis
- Counseling
- Narrative therapy

All of these psychological treatments can be used either as an alternative to medication or in combination with it. They tend to be more effective in addressing the causes of nonmelancholic depression. However, a thorough assessment of the sufferer is needed to decide on the best set of approaches.

COGNITIVE BEHAVIORAL THERAPY

People suffering from depression, particularly nonmelancholic depression, often have an ongoing negative view of themselves and the world around them. This negative way of thinking typically isn't confined to episodes of depression; rather, it's an ongoing part of how these people think about life. Many or all of their experiences are distorted through a negative filter, and their thinking patterns become so entrenched that they don't even notice the resulting thinking errors.

Cognitive behavioral therapy aims to show people how their thinking affects their mood and to teach them to think less negatively about life and themselves. It's based on the understanding that negative thinking is a habit that, like any other bad habit, can be broken. Cognitive behavioral therapy is conducted by trained therapists in either individual therapy or small groups. Homework may be assigned between sessions. Between six and ten sessions may be required, although the number will vary from person to person.

INTERPERSONAL THERAPY

The causes of depression or a vulnerability to developing depression can often be traced to personality and aspects of social functioning in areas such as work, relationships, and other social roles. Therefore, the underlying assumption of interpersonal therapy is that depression and interpersonal problems are related. In interpersonal therapy, the goal is to understand how these factors are operating in an individual's current life situation, and how they are involved in his or her depression and risk for future depression. Twelve to sixteen sessions of interpersonal therapy are usually required.

MINDFULNESS-BASED COGNITIVE THERAPY

Mindfulness-based cognitive therapy includes simple breathing meditations and yoga stretches to help participants become more aware of the present moment, including getting in touch with moment-to-moment changes in the mind and the body. It also includes basic education about depression and exercises from cognitive therapy that help people explore links between their thoughts and feelings. The aim is to teach people how best to care for themselves when depression threatens to overwhelm them. Mindfulness-based cognitive therapy has been used as a relapse prevention strategy with extremely encouraging results (Teasdale et al. 2000).

ACCEPTANCE AND COMMITMENT THERAPY

Acceptance and commitment therapy, one of the recently developed mindfulness-based behavior therapies, has been found effective in treating a diverse range of clinical conditions, including depression (Zettle and Rains 1989). In contrast to more typical assumptions regarding "healthy normality," acceptance and commitment therapy assumes that the psychological processes of a normal human mind often create psychological suffering. Based on the assumption that ongoing attempts to get rid of symptoms often actually create clinical disorders, symptom reduction isn't a goal of this form of therapy. Rather, the aim is to step back from instantaneous responses to situations and develop the capacity to observe that many experiences are just passing thoughts or feelings, not facts. Clients are taught to simply notice these experiences. This approach helps people recognize what they can't control, giving them more energy to focus on what they can control. It encourages people to live in the present, rather than the past or future, and to commit to actions that are consistent with their values and appropriate to the current situation.

The mantra of acceptance and commitment therapy is "Accept, commit, and take action." The purpose of this form of therapy is to give people greater flexibility in how they live and respond to various situations. It encourages them to take healthy action, even if they don't feel like it, and to stop doing things that are unhelpful. Being able to recognize what is healthful and what is harmful, and then take appropriate action, is probably one of the most important skills anyone can learn in these rapidly changing times.

PSYCHOANALYSIS

Psychoanalysis is an extended treatment, ranging from months to years in duration, in which a relationship is developed between the therapist and the patient. The relationship is then used to explore aspects of the person's experience in great depth. The assumption is that the supportive relationship between therapist and patient, along with working on understanding the links between past and present, can resolve depression and make the person less vulnerable to becoming depressed again.

COUNSELING

Counseling encompasses a broad set of approaches and skills that aim to help people explore problems and preferred solutions. Counseling can help people with long-standing problems in the family or at work, as well as with sudden major problems (crisis counseling).

NARRATIVE THERAPY

Narrative therapy is a form of counseling based on understanding the stories people use to describe their lives. The therapist listens to how the client presents problems as stories and then helps the person consider how these stories may be a barrier to overcoming difficulties. It sees problems as being separate from people and assists people in recognizing the range of knowledge and skills they already have but may not recognize, and how they can apply those strengths to problems in their lives.

Narrative therapy differs from other forms of therapy in that it puts a major emphasis on identifying an individual's strengths and highlighting evidence of how the person has mastered problems in the past. It seeks to build on people's resilience rather than focus on their negative experiences.

What Actually Works

You may be wondering what all of this information means for you and what you can do next. While this chapter summarizes the latest medical research about depression and its treatments, I'm acutely aware that simply listing the options doesn't illuminate a clear path forward. As I'll discuss in chapter 11, I believe that most researchers are trying to find helpful answers. Yet most research involves examining the relationships between a small number of parameters; for example, comparing one drug to another or to no treatment at all (a placebo), or comparing cognitive behavioral therapy to psychoanalysis. This can be helpful for making choices between different treatments. However, given that the World Health Organization (2001) projects that depression will be the second-most-disabling illness worldwide by 2020, it begs the question of whether researchers are missing something.

As someone who has been through depression, I believe that this research approach has some limitations in its capacity to help people and their doctors make meaningful decisions about treatment. While the current research approach can be beneficial, it needs to be supplemented with a more holistic perspective that can help us make decisions about how to integrate medical and lifestyle options.

In the Western world, depressed people tend to be highly stressed and short on time. They need guidance in how to allocate their time among approaches, from taking antidepressants or going into long-term psychotherapy to leaving a stressful job or ending a toxic relationship to exercising or practicing meditation and beyond. I believe that we can only know the answers to this question if we consider a person's whole life and provide advice based on what works best for similar people who have experienced depression. It seems that for many doctors, the default treatment is prescribing an antidepressant. Perhaps other strategies need to be considered just as seriously.

In chapter 11, Depression Treatments That Work, I summarize the findings of a survey of over four thousand people with depression or bipolar disorder in which I asked respondents to rate all the treatments they'd tried. I wasn't seeking to identify a single best therapy; rather, I wanted to understand which types of treatments helped the most. I then take this analysis into account and provide practical answers to the question, *What can I do today to start myself on the path toward long-term, sustainable recovery?* From my own experience, I know that hope is one of the most powerful elements in any recovery plan, so first, let's take a look at the stories of several people who have experienced the depths of depression and found a way out.

CHAPTER 2

PATRICK KENNEDY

Former US Representative

PATRICK KENNEDY IS THE YOUNGEST SON of the late US Senator Edward M. (Ted) Kennedy and nephew of President John F. Kennedy. He was born in Massachusetts into a large, extended, close-knit family. His mother suffered from severe depression and alcoholism that ran in her family, while his father suffered from profound effects of what we would today identify as post-traumatic stress disorder, or PTSD, caused by the murder of his two brothers (the assassinations of President John F. Kennedy and Robert F. Kennedy). Despite the prevalence of mental health concerns in the family, the times forbade them from speaking about their issues.

Patrick first noticed signs of depression in his early teens and was hospitalized at seventeen for cocaine addiction. While attending college, Patrick found a mentor in Frank DiPaolo, who essentially adopted Patrick as his grandson and played a crucial part in Patrick's recovery. During this time, Patrick joined the Democratic Party. He became a representative in Rhode Island's House of

Representatives at twenty years old and became the youngest member of the US Congress at twenty-seven.

He found the greatest satisfaction working on mental health reform in politics because of his life experiences. Patrick coauthored a major piece of legislation in 2008, the Mental Health Parity and Addiction Equity Act. In 2006, while working on this legislation, he had a breakdown stemming from alcohol and OxyContin addiction. He was too concerned about stigma to seek appropriate treatment. Patrick bears a dual diagnosis of bipolar II and addiction.

Because Patrick made his sobriety his main priority, he's now in recovery.

Patrick left Congress in 2011, married Amy Petitgout the same year, and has two young children. He cofounded One Mind for Research, a nonprofit foundation dedicated to solving the mysteries of the brain through unified research. Patrick remains an active mental health advocate.

Patrick, could you tell me about the best parts of your childhood?

My family. Growing up in a large extended family, who, when we were fortunate enough to be together, always enjoyed each other's company. Being a member of my family meant growing up in politics, working hard, and playing hard. My father instilled a great love of the sea and nature—through sailing, spending time at the beach, and camping.

My father's work with international refugees was extensive. My family and I often accompanied him on those trips. I had a front-row seat to political life and was able to watch his fight for social justice—the soul of his career. Naturally, my father was also a champion of health care reform. One of the ways he made a difference at the end of his career was endorsing a young senator named Barack Obama. He made a commitment to my father that he would push for improvements to health care, and he delivered on that. He honored my father and every single American who felt it was unjust and immoral to deny lifesaving care and treatment to another human being.

What did you enjoy so much about outdoor trips with your father?

I enjoyed the excitement and adventure of the outdoors. I love being near the ocean and live near it to this day. Sailing is a lifting experience which keeps my spirit afloat like many other outdoors events I enjoy with my family and friends. These experiences growing up were so important to my sense of well-being and place in the world. I witnessed the environment being a salvation for my father. He always gained sustenance from being out on the water, sailing, walking on the beach, and swimming in the ocean. I was fortunate to see the beach as a place where I could also recharge my batteries. The closeness he had with nature was a cherished gift that he shared with all of us.

Do you remember any difficulties in your early life?

When I was around thirteen, I was crying a great deal. I couldn't put my finger on exactly why I was, but it didn't feel like I was making friends. I was feeling isolated. I started using marijuana, cocaine, and alcohol when I was fourteen or fifteen. I asked to go away to boarding school as I thought it would afford me more freedom. I was hoping a different environment would change things for me. I'd sleep fourteen or fifteen hours a day, but still be tired most of the time. Then I'd have great bursts of energy and wouldn't need much sleep at all.

At seventeen, I was hospitalized for cocaine dependency. As time went on, I found other drugs to substitute, like alcohol, pain medication, amphetamines, and benzodiazepines. Self-medicating became a habit, and I soon suffered from the disease of addiction.

My father had seen his two brothers murdered, and those terrible events were repeatedly replayed on television. We didn't know what to call it back then, but he clearly suffered profound post-traumatic stress from those events and, consequently, self-medicated himself. Any time there was a loud sound, it threw him off—you could feel his anxiety. To cope, he tried to keep moving, to stay busy and preoccupied. His generation didn't slow down to reflect on troubled feelings. Introspection wasn't something viewed as masculine or acceptable. My father's generation did not talk about feelings. Certainly, mental illness was viewed as a sign of weakness, and you simply didn't ask for help.

My relationship with my mother was loving and supportive, but it was difficult and confusing to see her suffering with depression and alcoholism. She is a kind and beautiful woman who suffered with these illnesses for most of her life. The struggle that she also endured through our family tragedies was unfathomable.

I loved and adored my parents, but I suffered with them. When I was at college, there was an editorial in the local paper, the *Providence Journal*. The piece was a vicious personal critique of both of my parents. I remember taking it to heart, feeling defensive and enormously angry at the writer. Inwardly, I wanted to attack anybody who attacked them.

Did you fear for your father's safety when he ran for president in 1980?

Several times there were specific threats to him, which is why he had a bulletproof vest in his closet. We didn't understand it, but it wasn't anything we questioned. For security, we always had people around the house with guns. These things were normal for us. I traveled around with my father extensively; consequently, I also experienced people attacking him verbally. It was disconcerting to say the least, as my whole sense of self was so closely intertwined with my parents.

How did your parents' mental health issues impact the family?

In my family we weren't supposed to talk about it, because any weakness was viewed as a character flaw, not a brain chemistry issue. The shame of those illnesses was something I ended up carrying. I had a perfect storm of genetic predisposition and environmental factors to lead me down this same road. But I feel blessed for my life's experiences. My life and family have given me the great opportunity to work to change attitudes toward mental illness and try to eradicate the stigma associated with these illnesses. The blessing is, I can take my own experience, both as a politician and patient, to fight for a change in laws, as well as a change in attitudes.

What is your mother's diagnosis?

She suffers from severe depression—just intractable. She's had periods of great productivity, but they haven't been marked by the kind of mania you see in a more manic-depressive or bipolar illness. I've been diagnosed as bipolar II, so I'm not classic bipolar either.

What are your memories of how your mother's condition affected your family life?

It was the elephant in the room. You didn't acknowledge it. It was there and everybody knew it was there, but no one could see it for what it was. We all tried to keep it a secret, but of course it wasn't a secret. Everybody knew. But denial can be deep. Being in public life, as we were, the sense of shame was exacerbated because we lived when there was less understanding and acceptance of these issues. The combination of those factors made it enormously difficult for her. Having to worry about publicity just added insult to injury. The illness itself is an obstacle. To fight the illness with the isolation derived from stigma compounds the illness.

For high school you went to Phillips Academy?

Yes. I know people who look back on those days as the glory days, but I harbored a perfectionist aim and therefore always felt like I was falling short. I never felt as though I measured up. Adolescence exacerbated my insecurities and boosted my fears, rather than my self-confidence.

You were about fifteen when your parents divorced?

I was fourteen. My parents had been separated quite a while before they actually divorced, so it wasn't a traumatic event in terms of a sudden change in our lives. It was then my parents decided I should get counseling. They were concerned about the impact of the divorce.

Looking back, I was plagued by anxiety and inconsolable sadness. I had great difficulty coping, whereas it didn't seem my counterparts suffered as I did. Everybody goes through adolescent angst. Perhaps they did a better job hiding it. In retrospect, teachers and mentors took me under their wing in ways that illustrated their concern for my emotional stability.

Was there a reason for the sadness?

Even though it wasn't acknowledged, my parents' struggles were enormously difficult. The situations themselves were tragic enough, and then add the public rehashing. It wasn't hard for people who were total strangers to know I had a full plate. That was probably to my benefit, because people reached out to me who knew more about my situation than I could even acknowledge. I knew something wasn't working for me, but I couldn't put my finger on it. I just felt so isolated.

I thought our family had successfully kept all these secrets, and then one day I was in a bookstore and walked by the *K* section. I picked up a few of the books about my family and saw these things I thought were big secrets, never to be spoken of, written for all to see.

Were you able to confide in anyone?

In my home that wasn't permissible. I always worried if I spoke about my family, somehow it would reflect badly on them. I knew I wasn't being judged simply as Patrick; I was being judged as a member of my family. I took great pains not to tell anyone of my suffering because I was always concerned the story would spread. I knew sharing a normal story of the struggles I had with my parents and their difficulties wasn't just my story. It would easily become newsworthy. I was painfully aware of this at an early age.

You went from being hospitalized at seventeen to running for public office at twenty. That's a big turnaround. What do you attribute it to?

I was in college and needed to remake myself, even though I had barely achieved any sense of adulthood. I was already marked as damaged goods, and that fueled a desire to prove my worth in other ways—to prove (mostly to my father) that I could still do big things successfully. If you want to check how you're doing, there's nothing like running for elective office and having people vote on whether they like you or not. That's a pretty powerful validation of whether you're okay or not. For a long time, I looked for outside validation.

Do you remember specific strategies that you applied that helped you stay well between seventeen and twenty?

I went to 12-step meetings regularly. I was also adopted by an older gentleman, Frank DiPaolo. I didn't realize at the time how old he was, because he was extremely young at heart. He was over eighty when I met him, but he carried himself like he was in his sixties. He had a worldly way about him. He had a spiritual quality, soulfulness, that I was immediately attracted to. He became a surrogate grandfather to me. I'm so blessed to have had the privilege of knowing him. He really helped save my life because he was so old-school—a real upstanding guy. He worked extra jobs so he could put his four children through college even though he never went himself. He was a hard worker and masculine. He was everything I aspired to be, and I gravitated toward him. His unconditional love and acceptance of me was so sustaining.

I remember when my roommate from rehab sold his story to the *National Enquirer* for ten thousand dollars. I walked into our local grocery store, and on the newspaper rack, right where you come in, was a full-page picture of me with the headline "Patrick Kennedy

Cocaine Addict." You can imagine my horror. I was trying to put all that behind me, and I'd hoped I could keep my story under wraps. I was so shamed by it. I knew the cat was out of the bag.

When I went over to Frank's house, I was terrified about his response. I knew that this notion of me being a drug addict would be hard for him to accept and I was terrified about what it would mean for our relationship. I also really worried that I'd let him down. I felt like I'd betrayed him, and I was worried it would make him look like a chump because he supported this guy who was a loser.

I'll never forget him saying to me, "That rat." I knew what he meant right away. It's not at all what I expected him to say. He said, "How dare someone tell your private business." Although he didn't know how to talk about these issues of mental illness and addiction, he understood how shaming they were and so, therefore, if you had "problems," then they should be kept private. I still believe that while I welcomed his becoming my personal protector, I now see that it is this idea of keeping things "quiet" that poses the biggest obstacle to effective advocacy and progress in treating these as medical issues rather than moral ones.

How did you meet Frank?

It was just a random meeting. I was a skinny, nineteen-year-old Providence College student who was a refugee from Massachusetts. I didn't have any family in the neighborhood. I found myself going to this great little restaurant called the Castle Spa, and he was the proprietor. He had owned it for over forty years and made all the food.

I'm really intrigued by the randomness of the meeting. There's an old saying that "when the student is ready, the teacher will appear." Did you feel that was the case for you?

Absolutely. Frank changed my life. He taught by the way he lived. Frank became an emotional foundation and also a political foundation for me. I had huge credibility because of his credibility, politically and personally. I couldn't believe anyone could like me if they really knew me, but he really knew me and my struggles, and just continued to love and support me.

Frank obviously lived an extraordinary life. What's the single greatest life message he gave to you?

The number of years he lived, 106, is certainly remarkable. But the most remarkable thing about him was the way he lived those years. He lived in the moment. He was never preoccupied about things. I've struggled to live in the present. Part of my recovery today is endeavoring to live in the present—not the future, not the past, but right now. He seemed to do that so effortlessly, and he drew people to him because they loved being around him. It's a powerful thing. You know it when you see it. It's hard to describe, but it's that phrase "Stop and smell the roses." In other words, live a little bit; don't just let life pass you by. He lived that way every single day.

He grew tomato plants, and they were the biggest in the neighborhood. He grew sweet basil, which he would freeze so he could put it in his tomato soup in the middle of winter. This guy was grounded. He loved gardening, he loved his friends, he loved cooking, and he loved sharing a meal with people. These were new things to me. I didn't have that sense of how sacred breaking bread with someone was. Knowing him allowed me to have a much fuller life.

I saw him every day. What made it so profound was that it didn't have to be anything out of the ordinary or special; it was the continuity and consistency that made it so powerful for me. I never worried I was taking too much of his time. I've had a lot of important people around me and usually felt they could be doing something more substantial than spending time with me. Frank made me feel I was important to him, and he demonstrated that by spending a lot of time with me. There's just no substitute for it. So I feel blessed.

You also had a good relationship with your father, so how was Frank different?

Frank was around all the time. My dad was the most important connection I had in life, but he was a very busy person. He belonged to a lot of people. Frank was already in semiretirement mode by the time we met each other. He gave me time, and that was a huge commodity I couldn't get enough of.

Jumping forward now, what were the most stressful elements of political life for you?

The life you live in politics is self-centered and based on superficiality. I knew politics really well, and it came naturally to me. I knew how to live on the surface, how to put the face on. That was something I learned as a coping mechanism. I won all my elections, and I won them handily, even amidst great turmoil and scandals that would have sidelined most politicians. But that ability became a liability because it kept me from changing what I needed to.

If I was to change, I couldn't use the same skills I'd been using. Getting new skills while trying to live in the old familiar way wasn't conducive to change.

When my father passed away, it was a huge turning point in my life. I took that opportunity to change. I became introspective about living a different life. I was fortunate enough to have friends who encouraged me to take a leap of faith, and of course I was very blessed to run into Amy, my wife. As it turns out, she has been the perfect partner on this journey.

What's the thing you're most proud of from your time in politics?

Definitely working on the Mental Health Parity and Addiction Equity Act. As well as it being a great legislative and political victory, it was a personal victory because I got to do it with my father. My father tended to resist talking about and acknowledging these issues, like many of his generation. He was loathe to acknowledge mental illness, which had been incorrectly perceived as a character issue, instead of a chemistry issue.

So, the fact I was able to have him be the primary sponsor in the senate was a great personal vindication for me. Even though he never got entirely comfortable with the issue, he understood the politics of it and the fact that it marked a paradigm shift his son had played a part in creating. He could acknowledge as a politician that I was doing something big, even though he wasn't sure how comfortable he was with it.

The act wasn't passed until 2008. Jim Ramstad and I had been fighting for its passage for our whole political careers. Fortunately for the cause, the bill passed just before health care reform got taken up. If it had been part of that bill, it probably would have been bargained away. It would have been dropped from the final bill because it was so hard to get a consensus on health care reform.

There was resistance not only from the insurance industry but also from the mental health community. Some of our biggest opponents were among us, as is often the case. There are some in our community who believe there ought to be equality of insurance coverage for "biologically" based brain illnesses, such as bipolar disorder or schizophrenia, but not for affective disorders such as addictions, which are biological too but less politically acceptable.

The biggest struggle we had wasn't with the insurance industry; it came from our own inability to unify around a common principle, that we were all in this together. We all deal with the same stigma in one form or another, due to the illness originating in the brain, as opposed to any other organ in the body.

While you were working so hard on this, you had a meltdown yourself in 2006, with alcohol and OxyContin addiction. Did the stress of working on the act contribute to that?

Ironically, my situation got out of hand because I didn't want to seek the very treatment that I was advocating for due to the stigma. I was fighting that battle both politically and personally. I couldn't have foreseen the silver lining at the time, but after I went to treatment, many of my legislative colleagues in Congress wrote me get-well notes. When I returned to Congress, I visited many of them, and they often talked to me about their own struggles, because now I was the public face of addiction. In addition to being personally rewarding, that also served a very important political purpose; it made it hard for them to ignore either me or the bill, as both I and they knew it was personal to us both.

What components have been important to your recovery?

I'm a big believer in cognitive behavioral therapy, which evidence shows is very effective. You've got to act your way into different thinking. That's what changes not only your perspective but also your brain wiring. You've got to go against the grain and what comes naturally. The best way to change your brain chemistry is to do different things than you were doing in the past. That's not always easy. Because these are new things, they create anxiety.

I've learned these lessons from my peers who are also in recovery. I attend 12-step recovery support groups daily because they help me recenter my thinking, like cognitive behavioral therapy does. Through a slow but steady change in your actions on a day-to-day basis, you see changes in your thinking. The emotional support the 12-step fellowship provides me is very powerful. I also think having an intimate relationship with someone who knows you completely, accepts you completely, and loves you completely, is absolutely foundational. I have a wife and two children, and they have been enormously grounding and very helpful in keeping me on track. Getting enough sleep and exercise has also been extremely helpful for me to remain healthy in both body and mind.

Why do you think the 12-step approach works?

I subscribe to the belief the illness I face is not just a physical allergy (in AA, alcoholism is referred to as an allergy because of the pervasive nature of the ailment), it's also a mental obsession and a spiritual malady. It's a three-pronged illness. So just getting medicine and medical care for the physical aspect isn't enough. For the mental obsession part, you need to work on your psychosocial behavior so you can change the outcomes of your behavior by changing the way you relate to the world.

The spiritual element is fundamental because you need to have a sense of belonging, and [the] recognition [that] you're not the center of the universe. Real liberation in life comes from being part of a community, as opposed to being an individual. That's liberating because you no longer think of your life as some arbitrary existence, and instead feel you have a purpose. You are connected to a larger whole, and that's really powerful.

How does the transition from "me" to "we" happen in the 12-step group environment?

It's different for everybody. We all come to these realizations in our own time, and when we do, we realize that not only are we not alone but we now have a solution to our problems—and the great paradox is that when we help others, we get better too. That's part of our mission once we're in recovery: spreading the notion that there is another way of living. Not everyone is ready to hear that message, but we can make it available to people who are ready. We have to be examples by how we live, and ready to share what we know.

How did you meet Amy, your wife?

I met her at a dinner honoring my Aunt Eunice, who was the founder of Special Olympics. It was a dinner for the ARC of New Jersey. (ARC stands for Association of Retarded Citizens. As you know, these days we don't use the word "retarded," so it's known simply by its acronym, ARC.) My wife's father is a retired special education teacher and has worked in the intellectual disability movement his whole life. Of course, he knew about this dinner and bought a few tickets to it. At the last minute he decided not to go and gave his ticket to Amy. I saw her at the dinner and was interested in seeing her again, so I made every effort to do so.

Over the course of the next year we got to know each other better, and then I left Congress. The next spring I asked her to marry me. I had decided I was going to start living another kind of life, and I recognized in Amy the kind of qualities I was really attracted to. In addition to being a beautiful woman, she's got a maturity about her that was very attractive to me. Amy and our two children now bring a groundedness that guides me and keeps me in the present.

You also mentioned that exercise has been helpful. What type of exercise do you do, and was it hard to get started?

I started jogging, and I now alternate between jogging and swimming. I also share a trainer with my wife to do some light weights. I want to incorporate it into my daily life. That's my game plan. I don't want to try to do too much because I don't want to stop doing it. I exercise every day, more for my brain than for my body. I get a real sense of stability in my life from the endorphins that come from the exercise.

In addition to the things you've mentioned—cognitive behavioral therapy, support groups, Amy and the kids, and exercise—are there any other elements that keep you well?

I'm working on eating right. I'm conscious that you are what you eat, and if you eat a lot of processed foods full of nasty chemicals, they won't be good for you in the long run, even if they make you feel good. I'm interested in learning about better nutrition and incorporating it into my life because I know that will help with my brain chemistry. I try to eat lots of fruit and protein and cut down on the refined sugar and caffeine. I haven't had much success, but my goal is progress, not perfection. I also try to get regular sleep, which is indispensable to good mental health.

How important is medication for you?

Medication has been a big part of my life up until r
I've been concentrating on support groups, exerc
eating right, I have been able to wean myself off of it with the help of a physician. I still have moments when I feel out of sorts, but I can now recognize those moments because I'm surrounded by folks who are constants in my life. I don't have the fear of falling off the edge of the earth when those feelings come over me. I can take some deep breaths. I can live a routine that grounds me.

I've been off medication for about two years, and this is not necessarily a permanent decision. Right now it's something I'm trying out.

In his 2012 book A *First-Rate Madness,* psychiatrist Nassir Ghaemi says that, after studying John F. Kennedy's medical files, he believes he had a hyperthymic personality, which is often linked to bipolar disorder. Did you sense that he or other members of your family might have bipolar disorder?

These are modern terms, and to ascribe them to folks who lived during a different time and place would be a projection. It's clear my uncle nearly died at times because of his Addison's disease, and he saw adversity through his war experience and the deaths of his brother, Joseph, and his sister, Kathleen. The pain he suffered, both physically and emotionally, gave him a depth and wisdom far beyond his years. So even though he was the youngest president, he conveyed a level of depth and wisdom that made him a natural leader at a time when America was looking for someone to give it a sense of direction.

Ghaemi concluded, in his book, [that] people who have gone through mental illness or suffering have greater empathy and perspective, making them well suited to leading in times of crisis, and that was certainly the case with my uncle. He was the right person for the right time. His sense of destiny drove him in a way that made him ideally suited to be president at that time.

My uncle was the first president to address civil rights as a moral cause on national television. He said, "Who among us would be content to have the color of his skin changed…and be content with the counsels of patience and delay?" That was a moral appeal for people to think about how they lived in a country where people were still being denied basic human rights because of the color of their skin. I feel the same passion to eliminate stigma associated with mental illness. Some people's genetics cause them to be discriminated against because of their brain illness. Mental illness is a question of chemistry, not a question of character.

We need to take a page from my uncle's playbook and think about how we would like to be treated if it was us, or our mother or father or sister or brother, who was suffering from one of these illnesses. Do we think the status quo is acceptable? I think that's a rhetorical question similar to the one my uncle posed fifty years ago, and it applies just as poignantly to the cause of mental illness. I feel blessed I'm able to be in recovery, and that part of my recovery is being part of a movement—part of a "we," not just me. There's great salvation in that.

In his book, Ghaemi looks at outstanding leaders in the past who had a mental illness, such as Abraham Lincoln and Winston Churchill. Do you think someone with an acknowledged mental illness could reach the highest office today?

I don't think our political system would allow for it in the modern world, where every detail of people's past and their behaviors are dissected. Unfortunately, we get pigeonholed so fast. In this age of instantaneous news, twenty-four-hour surveillance, and the politics of personal destruction, it's very unlikely that mistakes won't become the lead story. Politics today would probably limit the ability of the leaders like those you mentioned to survive politically in modern times, in spite of their obvious abilities.

Tell me about One Mind for Research, the organization you cofounded.

One Mind is an independent, nonprofit organization dedicated to curing diseases of the brain and eliminating the stigma and discrimination associated with mental illness and brain injuries. I was inspired by my uncle's famous moon shot speech and his challenge to the country. The success that came from it was extraordinary, and I've used it as a metaphor for what we can do in this new quest to understand how the brain works.

Traveling to the moon was seemingly beyond our reach, especially in 1961. On the fiftieth anniversary of his challenge, I wanted to create a mission to understand how the galaxy of brain neurons works. Because JFK was such a bold and big thinker, I thought his inspiration could still be utilized today. Instead of just looking back on that anniversary and saying how great it was, we could be reenergized by setting and achieving new goals we never thought were possible.

There appear to be a lot of benefits and also drawbacks to being a Kennedy. On balance, do you consider it to be a blessing or a burden?

It's a blessing in every single way you could imagine. Life is life, and there are challenges for everybody. I live with gratitude that I've had the life that I've had because I realize I wouldn't be the person I am today without all of those life experiences. I also realize that in serving others I can be freed from the bondage of self to live a life beyond my wildest dreams.

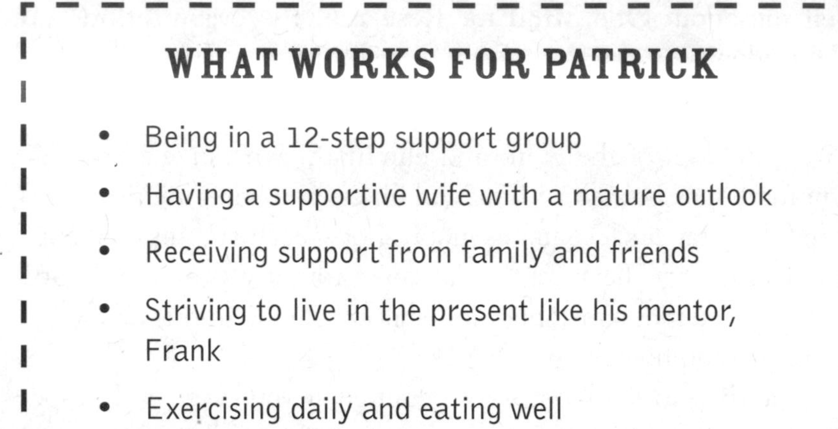

WHAT WORKS FOR PATRICK

- Being in a 12-step support group
- Having a supportive wife with a mature outlook
- Receiving support from family and friends
- Striving to live in the present like his mentor, Frank
- Exercising daily and eating well
- Getting sufficient sleep
- Finding meaning in mental health advocacy

CHAPTER 3

TRISHA GODDARD

TV Talk Show Host and Mental Health Advocate

TRISHA GODDARD, BORN IN ENGLAND IN 1957, was the eldest of four daughters of a woman from Dominica. Until she was in her fifties, she believed that her mother's white husband was her biological father, only to discover otherwise. Not surprisingly, she always had an unnerving feeling of being different. The family moved to Tanzania and then back to England before Trisha moved to the Middle East, where she worked as a flight attendant. During this time, an Australian passenger pursued her relentlessly and convinced her to move to Australia, and they subsequently married.

During her time in Australia, Trisha had two failed marriages, a terrible depressive episode, and a suicide attempt, and also endured the horror of her sister's suicide. She also became the first black person to host a prime-time current affairs show on television, hosted a children's TV program, ran her own production company, and was a government advisor on mental health before finding true love and a happy third marriage.

In 1998, she was invited to return to the United Kingdom to host her own show: ITV's award-winning *Trisha Goddard* show, which focused on issues around relationships, conflict resolution, and mental health. Many people christened her the United Kingdom's Oprah. In 2008, she was diagnosed with breast cancer, which is now in remission. In 2012, she was asked to move to the United States to host NBC's *The Trisha Goddard Show.* She has worked with a number of charities to help reduce the stigma around mental illness and is the author of *Trisha: A Life Less Ordinary* (2009).

Trisha, could you tell me what it was like growing up in England in a mixed-race family?

There were no other families of color around, so the only range of colors was my family. When I was a little kid, it was all right. Then we went to East Africa, which was idyllic. There were kids from Australia, New Zealand, Africa, and all over. In one classroom, there'd be a five-year-old in one corner and an eighteen-year-old in the next.

Did you receive a good education despite having such a huge range of ages?

Yes. We learned French from age five, and we learned Latin. My sisters and I were way ahead of our peer group when we came back to England. We returned to Norfolk for about three to six months, but it was horrific. I was literally greeted at the school by children chanting, "Nigger, nigger," and I was beaten up on a daily basis. One teacher told me, "You've got to learn to put up with this, because we people don't want you here." It was the first time I felt terribly bullied.

Were you able to talk with anyone about that, such as your parents?

I told my mother. She went up to the school, but I don't think it made any difference. Much later, in 1994 when I was in a psychiatric hospital, all of that stuff, which I had forgotten, came back, and I realized that I was probably more deeply affected by what happened than I realized at the time. Luckily, my father, who was a psychiatric nurse, got a job at a mental hospital in Surrey. Going from Norfolk to Surrey meant going from a rural area to a much more enlightened, wealthy area full of airline pilots. When we walked into the classroom the first day to meet the new teacher, he was a Sri Lankan gentleman, and I remember thinking that was fantastic. Later, I was one of the first black girls to go to my very well-heeled high school. I was lucky that I was so bright. I loved being at my school.

Was that the first time you felt you had good friends in a school environment?

I had good friends in my primary school once we moved to Surrey. I was always one of those kids who didn't have loads and loads of good friends. I wasn't popular enough to be with the popular ones, wasn't geeky enough to be with the geeky ones, and wasn't sporty enough to be with the sporty ones. I always felt like I didn't fit in. I also felt that within my family because I looked different. This made sense later, when I found that the man I had been convinced was my father wasn't my biological father.

As I understand it, you had a close and warm relationship with the man you thought was your father, and then it became distant?

When I was little, he was my hero, but then when we were in East Africa, the feeling of distance started. When we came back to England—thank God I loved high school so much, because I didn't like being at home. My father used to smack us, but it went beyond that. When he lost his temper, I felt I had to protect my sisters. Both of my parents were doing night duty as psychiatric nurses, and they wanted to sleep during the day. If my sisters woke either of them up, I was always the one to be punished. I always took responsibility.

My father used to call me "bloody bastard's child." The swearing was frightening, and he was extremely aggressive. One time my mother found him laying into me and screamed, "Stop, stop! You'll kill the child!" I learned to completely dissociate from pain. When he was beating [the] hell out of me, I would go somewhere else in my head.

When you look back on your childhood now, did you feel loved?

Up to about the age of five, very much so. I used to change the lyrics "I Want to Be Bobby's Girl" to "I Want to Be Daddy's Girl." What saved me is what distanced me from him: that I was very bright. I passed my 11-plus test at the end of primary school with very high marks, so I was offered a place at a good secondary school.

What was great about high school?

I had a wonderful teacher who took an interest in me. I used to write a lot of poetry about how I felt and what I was going through, and she was the only person I showed it to. It was so deep and dark. My friends couldn't have understood it, but she absolutely got it. On her recommendation, I sent some of my poems to a radio show hosted by Alan Freeman, who used to read three poems from three different listeners during each show. One day he said, "I'm going to devote this day's poet's call to one writer." He read my poems on air, and I got loads of fan mail. I think I was about fourteen at the time.

What were the poems about?

The poems were all about death and loss, which was weird because the only person I knew of who had died at that time was my grandmother—my mother's mother in the West Indies—and I'd never met her. In retrospect, when I look at that poetry, I was clearly experiencing one of my many bouts of depression, but I didn't have a label for it then. I also had a lot of very obsessive behavior centering around the number four. I couldn't stand on the fourth stair, and I had to touch the water taps four times. Hardly anyone knew about OCD in 1971. This trait didn't last a long time, and I was never officially diagnosed with OCD or treated for it.

Beyond how your poetry reflected underlying depression, did you have any other symptoms of depression, such as insomnia?

Oh god, me and sleep. At three thirty in the morning, I'd think of something and become introspective about it, going over it again and again. I called it skidding. But my obsessions were pretty damn strong then. If I didn't touch things four times, then I didn't allow myself to eat anything more than a digestive biscuit. I don't believe I had an eating disorder. I don't like the term "eating disorder." I think of it as "eating distress."

It's said that women who have a violent father or family often end up in abusive relationships. Why do you think that is?

It happens because we learn confusing messages about what it means to be cared for or looked after. My father did work hard and provide for me. There are no two ways about it. Both of my parents worked like troopers, and I thank them for my work ethic. But I learned that being cared for includes violence. If violence is part of that package, you're not surprised when you get into other relationships and it remains part of the package. There also may be a chance that you attract men with a violent streak. I know that once I went through therapy, all sorts of people who were either mentally or physically abusive ran screaming from me.

What about the period where you were a flight attendant for Gulf Air? It sounds like that was party time.

I loved Gulf Air. Yeah, it was party time. I earned a lot of money, but I also worked flat out and saved up my leave time to take journalism courses. It was work hard, play hard, and it was the early days in the Middle East. I loved working in the Middle East, and I love Middle Eastern people.

What was your mental health like during that period?

Sometimes very giddy, sometimes very bad. In those days, there were no workers' rights. If we were overweight, we'd get put on the "fatties list." Three times on the fatties list and you were repatriated. It meant losing a lot of money, and I had a mortgage. I got put on the fatties list. In those days, we used to work a flight to Bangkok, where we'd buy speed. Speed is an especially bad idea if you have a predisposition to depression. Around that time, I got into a relationship with a violent boyfriend—no surprises there. I used to smoke a lot of dope and then, in between, I'd take a lot of speed. I went through some pretty mad stages and tough times.

What made you decide to leave Gulf Air?

I had gotten pretty sick of it, and I met an Australian man on the aircraft—Robert Nestdale. I think I was looking for an out and found one in Robert, who I ended up marrying. Don't ask me why. What a mistake that was.

It sounds as though he was a very controlling man.

Yeah. And I basically married somebody I didn't know. He had his own agenda. He was the first one to tell me there was talk about him being gay, but according to him, he wasn't. During the time we were together, I thought I was going mad. He was very skillful at getting information from my friends by pretending to be concerned for me. That relationship ended with my suicide attempt, which led to a lot of microsurgery for my injuries. I ended up addicted to Demerol. I realized that if I was going to stay alive, I had to get out of there. I had a friend who took me up to an ashram at Mangrove Mountain, a rural area north of Sydney. I stayed up there for a week. Then I left my husband and, at about the same time, started working for the Special Broadcasting Service, or SBS, an Australian multicultural public broadcasting service.

You had lots of reservations going into the marriage. What made you go forward?

Well, he was older. I guess I saw him as a grown-up with some stability. It's very difficult for me to work out why. Maybe I needed a parachute. He pursued me romantically, relentlessly. I was flattered by that. When I visited Australia, I loved it. He had some great friends, and some of them remain my friends. But I was truly a different person then, and I quickly found it wasn't working.

How long did the marriage last?

We were married in December. By about March or April I was in another bedroom, and by August I was in the hospital.

Was the suicide attempt just an impulse in the moment, or had you been thinking for a while that suicide was the only way out?

I had a real problem showing anger because of how much violence and aggression I had seen. I really believe at that time, if I hadn't gone for myself with the knife, I would have gone for Robert. The anger had been building up. I'd had one or two glasses of wine, but no more than that. It was just this buildup and an absolute scream of anger. I think I knew in that split second that the knife had to go either into me or into him. Ultimately, I couldn't do that to somebody else. So I turned it on myself, which, as I've learned from therapy, is something I did a lot. After time away from Robert, I knew the marriage was over and it was time to start a new life.

How did you meet your second husband?

I met Mark at SBS. He was a tape editor. We started going out when I was hosting the *7.30 Report,* a current affairs show. When my sister Linda killed herself in England, her death triggered two things in me: the desire to have a child, and the desire to start working against the injustices and stigma people with mental illness experience. That made me want to get up and shriek it, and I did get involved in mental health. It also made me think about why I wanted a baby. Like a lot of people struggling with death, I think I saw it as a way to renew life.

When did you become aware that your sister Linda had schizophrenia?

When she was about nineteen. I was four years older than her, and I flew back to London quite often. I'd get letters or telephone calls from my mom saying that Linda had disappeared again or had a breakdown. Another sister had a breakdown as well. I'd come back and be the fixer. I had misconceptions about what mental illness and schizophrenia were about then. Back then, I had no idea that what I used to go through was depression. I thought that was just me being me.

It's interesting that even though your parents were both psychiatric nurses, there was unease about discussing Linda's condition.

Definitely. Later, when I chaired the National Community Advisory Group on Mental Health in Australia, we found that some of the highest rates of stigma came from mental health professionals. When you ask a mental health professional what they'd do if they became ill themselves, many say they wouldn't tell their colleagues. It's very ironic.

In your work to help reduce the stigma of mental illness, what sort of things have you done?

I didn't start off planning to make a difference. Journalists would ask me why I'd been back in the United Kingdom for six weeks, and a publicist had advised me not to say anything about the mental stuff—to just say "illness." When asked, I'd say what a wonderful kid my sister had been, that she wrote poetry, and, oh yes, she had schizophrenia as well. I talked about it and ended up getting huge support.

I channeled my anger and frustration at what my sister had been through and realized I could actually do something. I was approached by Anne Deveson, an Australian journalist and mental health activist, and eventually became chair of the National Community Advisory Group on Mental Health, a position I held for ten years.

Going back to your second marriage, you eventually had a crisis and breakdown, your marriage was shaky, and your daughter Madison was dangerously ill. You had a real confluence of events, didn't you?

Running my production company with Mark, my second husband, was all-consuming. I was one of those people who never stood still for a moment because when I did, things got very scary.

I was only sleeping about three hours a night. Didn't everybody? And I became more and more and more busy. When I give presentations at banks, I warn people about this. I say, "Please don't be stereotypical of what depression looks like." For many, many people, depression means not washing or sitting in a dark corner doing nothing. In the world of business, depression often shows up as working and running so fast.

Amidst all of this frenetic activity, you discovered that your husband was having an affair with one of the employees of your production company. You overdosed and ended up in Northside Clinic. When you came to and realized you were in a psychiatric hospital, what were your thoughts?

I think I was angry. I never ask people if they're suicidal. I think it's a dumb question. I just wanted the pain to stop. I wanted the obsessing to just shut the hell up. I would have taken anything to stop it. If you handed me anything and said it would shut my head up for a minute, that's what I wanted. I wanted oblivion. So when I'm talking to people, I ask, "Do you just want to get out or escape? Would you do anything to get away from how you're feeling?" If they say yes, that usually translates to suicide risk or very severe risk-taking behavior.

Could you tell me about the relaxation therapy you undertook as part of your recovery?

It taught me that I could be quiet and still, and that there was a way of doing it where I didn't have to be frightened of doing nothing. It taught me another way of being. I found it an important addition to exercise.

You're very disciplined about exercise, aren't you?

I need exercise. And I can use it to help my mood. If my stress is up, I know what I need. It's like any of my medications. But it's important to be clear that I'm not slaving away in a gym—I'm outside. I have a firm belief that our mental health, as a population, has deteriorated the further away from nature we've gotten. We weren't meant to be under artificial lighting and in central heating or air-conditioning all the time. I believe we need green, we need to be outside. That's what I need.

How did you meet your third husband, Peter?

I knew of him because of the work he was doing in mental health. In those days, when I was chair of the National Community Advisory Group on Mental Health, we used to get a lot of papers from psychiatrists and people in the mental health field that might as well have been written in a foreign language. But Peter's papers were very easy to read. He assumed that doctors and the system should be tailored to the needs of the patient, and that was revolutionary in those days. When he was working on the Australian national mental health standards, I was part of a panel that interviewed him, and this led to his appointment and a number of subsequent meetings between us.

What was it that attracted you to him?

Well, he hates me saying this, but initially I was interested in him as a person and his passion about mental health. Frankly, so many people in the mental health services in those days were kind of burnt-out. It was a meeting of the minds, with both of us having a passion for mental health services and wanting to change people's thinking. That's where the attraction started for both of us. When people say, "I can't find a partner," I always tell them to join a volunteer organization and show that they're passionate about something. And anyone you meet who's going that extra mile for something they believe in is worth marrying.

You mention in your book that even though Peter is your third husband, you consider this your only true marriage. What do you mean by that?

Because of my depression, my breakdown, and all the psychotherapy I went through, I knew that I couldn't continue my cycle of self-destructive behavior. With Peter, it was the first time I got into a relationship where I went in with a checklist of what I needed to help make sure I wasn't being drawn back to the same sort of destructive types I'd been involved with before. I experienced it differently on every single level, which is why I always say it's my first marriage.

Was that an important part of the continuing improvement in your mental health?

Definitely. Because of the work I was doing and through knowing Peter, I read a lot of papers on depression. We used to get invited to caregiver and consumer conferences to give the perspectives of both sides. Peter, who would support me when I was having a tough time, said, "Hang on. I don't see myself as a caregiver." I think a lot of people don't get engaged or feel supported because we use these labels: "caregiver" or "consumer."

Why do you think you've been good for each other?

We always joke that the old me wouldn't have been interested in Peter, and that he wouldn't have been interested in the old me. Peter loved that I was a parent and the way I approached being a single parent. We share a passion for active parenting. It changes from week to week, moment to moment. If you want the next generation to be cognizant of their mental health, then parenting is something you'll need to focus on.

When you were offered the opportunity to return to the United Kingdom to host your own show, what sort of content did you want to present?

I inherited the staff from a show called *Vanessa*, and they gave me some of her tapes to look at. One of them was on eating disorders, and Vanessa was talking to a guy with anorexia. She tried to coax him into eating by laying on a guilt trip. I was horrified.

I was quite firm in telling the staff what the show was going to be like. I said, "These are my passions. I'm not burning my mental health credentials for anybody. If you don't like it, leave now." A few did. We completely retrained the staff. When Peter eventually became CEO of Norwich Mind, a mental health charity in the United Kingdom, I got him and his staff to come in and do some training with my team about their own mental health and that of our guests, and what to look out for.

Over the first year we changed the show a lot, and the kind of staff we attracted were people who had what I call "life history." We attracted guests with real traumas, and we probed beneath the surface. Being a journalist, I know that tabloid headlines bring the audience in. That's something I always used to say when I was working in mental health in Australia: "Make the headlines tabloid, and then when you've got people reading the story, slip in the mental health angle so they won't even notice it." It's all about positioning.

And that is indeed what we did. Over the years, lots of surveys have shown that many people learned about safe sex, relationships, and mental health from our show. It's rewarding to play a role in educating young people without them even realizing it.

What do you consider to be the highlights of those twelve years?

Making people think about mental health. You can't ram it down people's throats. It has to be a drip feed. You have to introduce it and make it normal and natural. I've heard anecdotally that the show started many, many conversations.

You were diagnosed with breast cancer in 2008. Was it a lump that first alerted you?

No. I cross-country run for my health. That's my thing that I do every day. I had a series of spectacular falls because I run through woods and other natural areas. I had injured my leg or my knee, I was having physical therapy, and I kept breaking my toe. I kept running and just didn't care. So the physical therapist sent me for some X-rays, and just out of courtesy, they asked whether I'd ever had a mammogram and then how long it had been since my last one. I couldn't remember, so they looked it up and told me I was due for another one.

What impact did your breast cancer diagnosis have?

It's hard to remember, because I wasn't looking at the big picture then. I cried for about three seconds, and then thought, *Bloody hell, what's next?* It's really hard. I don't know how I got through what I got through, and I think that's one of the wonderful things that the mind does. If my mental health ever had a test, that was it, and I passed with flying colors. You live minute by minute, hour by hour, day by day. I thought, *My god! I eat well, I don't smoke, and I don't drink much.* There's a tendency to keep looking for a reason. But then I thought, *Well, someone's got to be a statistic. If you were a statistic with depression, there's no reason why you can't be a statistic with breast cancer.* Those were scary, horrible times, and the sleeping tablet became my friend.

You mentioned that the time when you had cancer was a huge test of your mental health. What do you think kept you on track?

Depression was far more isolating than cancer and way scarier. Not that it diminishes your fears of mortality and so on, but I had a good family structure. A lot of the kind of baggage I'd dealt with in the past wasn't there with my cancer diagnosis. I had my daughters and Peter at home—what I consider to be my first true home. I got up in front of my staff and told them, "You're all very sweet, and you're all asking me how I am, and there's eighty of you. If this keeps up, I'm going to throttle somebody. They laughed, and then I said, "Look, if I'm at work, I'm all right. The best thing you can do is treat me as normal; then I'll feel more normal."

When and how did you find out that the man you thought was your father wasn't your biological father?

He told Peter long after my mum died in 2004, and of course Peter told me. I had a DNA test done as well, to see what my genetic makeup was. That revealed that it was highly unlikely that he'd been my father. It was something I'd suspected all my life, and when I found out, it was like a thousand pieces of a jigsaw puzzle fell into place.

You've had your own experiences. You've been married to Peter for seventeen years and obviously heard his perspective. And you've interviewed thousands of people about their mental health. What do you think are the best strategies to optimize mental health?

The starting point is to realize you have a state of mental health, and that you can support it by eating well, exercising, not drinking to excess, and not burning the candle at both ends continuously. The extreme end of that continuum is mental illness. It's not something to be frightened of. It's just like eating. If you eat too much of the wrong foods, you can become obese. But that doesn't mean you have to be frightened of being obese. It's just being aware of the consequences of certain behaviors.

There is no shame in telling someone that you have a problem. The shame might last for thirty seconds, during the time it takes to explain your dilemma. The old saying "A stitch in time saves nine" applies to both physical health and mental health.

What would your advice be to new parents about nurturing their child's mental health?

If you're a parent, you have tremendous power to optimize the next generation's mental health. It's not all about praising everything they do. It's also about avoiding name-calling and bullying your kids. It's about having conversations with your partner or a friend. I'm a great fan of parenting, and especially of mother-and-toddlers groups. I think they're very powerful for letting you know that if you're struggling, you're not the only one. Many women put a lot of pride in being a parent and think that there's something wrong if they ask for help. I'd say to them, "There is no shame in asking for help. You're less likely to get into big problems if you deal with them when they're small."

Thank you, Trisha. It's been fantastic learning about the road you've traveled and how you've applied those lessons to the wider world.

I'm still shocked when people recognize who I am. I've got a good family life now, and that keeps me safe.

WHAT WORKS FOR TRISHA

- Having a supportive romantic relationship and a family that keeps her grounded
- Knowing herself and not just trying to please others
- Exercising regularly and taking care of herself physically
- Spending time in nature
- Learning how to relax
- Seeking help early if something is amiss
- Helping others by sharing her story
- Advocating for people who can't advocate for themselves

CHAPTER 4

ALASTAIR CAMPBELL

Chief Advisor to Former UK Prime Minister Tony Blair

AS A YOUNG JOURNALIST, ALASTAIR CAMPBELL was on an assignment in Scotland when he had a breakdown related to excessive drinking and an unrelenting workload and was hospitalized due to psychosis. He decided to quit drinking, and after a relatively quick recovery, he returned to journalism before going to work for UK Opposition Leader Tony Blair, first as a press secretary, then as official spokesperson, and finally as director of communications and strategy when Blair became prime minister.

Alastair was credited with gaining support for Tony Blair's Labour Party from the traditionally conservative UK press, which many people believe was a key element in Blair's first election victory. Alastair rose to extraordinary influence within the government and was a major contributor to UK policy and communication while working in Opposition from 1994 to 1997 and in government from 1997 to 2003.

Alastair was a key figure in relations between the United Kingdom and the United States. President Bill Clinton once sent him a joking note saying he'd gotten Blair's permission to swap him for his own press secretary. President George Bush sponsored him to run in the London Marathon to raise money for research into leukemia, the disease that took Alastair's best friend's life. He also played an important role in the United Kingdom's decision to join the United States in the Iraq War.

During his time working with Blair, Alastair kept a comprehensive diary, which became the book *The Blair Years* (2007), a book that reached the top of the *Sunday Times* best seller list. His role in government was portrayed in the movies *The Queen* and *The Special Relationship*. During his heady days he struggled with depression, but only after he left his full-time role in government did he seek help and see a psychiatrist. He now leads a full life as a speaker and media commentator, but he says that the most rewarding work he does is helping break down the stigma of mental illness. He lives with his partner Fiona Millar, with whom he has three grown children, loves the outdoors, and is an avid supporter of the Burnley Football Club.

Alastair, could you tell me the best thing about your childhood?

The things that come straight to mind are my school, which I always liked, the countryside around us, my cycling and running, but especially my football.

What are the most memorable occasions from your childhood?

Quite a lot of them have to do with football. I used to go to games with my dad. I've always had a sense of anticipation and enjoyment about football. It became a ritual. I also have a lot of good memories of school. I can remember learning to write and that feeling when I first got it and understood what it was all about, at about four or five.

Do you still have any contact with friends from that time?

Only one, a guy called John Bailey. He was from a different background. My dad was a veterinarian, and we lived in a nice house. John was much more working class. I don't go back to that area much now because I've got no family there anymore, but I do keep in touch with him.

Were there any difficulties in that period?

The usual sort of sibling issues. Once my older brother Donald was chasing me and I slammed a door on him. It was a glass door and he put his arm through it. It was just horrific. He received a deep cut literally an inch from a main artery on his wrist. I was always getting in a lot of scrapes. The house opposite us had a big garage with a glass roof. I had this crazy idea of climbing up it, and I went through it. But beyond those sorts of things, nothing much.

I wanted to be the best at school. That was important to me. I was quite driven even at an early age.

When I was about ten, my dad had a bad accident and was in hospital for a long time. He was vaccinating some piglets and was attacked by the sow. She was meant to be locked up, but she got out and battered him against a wall. He was in a bad way for a long time and eventually gave up his practice as a vet. He joined the Ministry of Agriculture for a quieter life, and he was moved to Leicester when I was eleven.

How was high school for you?

It was weird arriving midterm. I remember being uncomfortable. Sport was still important, and I had quite a lot of action. I broke my leg twice and broke my arm playing rugby. Most of my holidays were spent up in Scotland. I never allowed myself to belong at school; I was always a bit of an outsider. I wore my Burnley scarf at school, and my teachers used to try to make me take it off. But it was from my life in the north and I didn't want to give that up, so I never took it off. I worked hard though.

And then off to Cambridge?

Yes. Leaving home wasn't a problem, but I didn't like Cambridge. I didn't like the whole class thing. Although my dad was a vet and I was middle class, I didn't feel I had much in common with most of the people at Cambridge. I didn't like the upper-class lot, the privately educated. I've never liked private schools. I think I was just at a bad age, to be honest. Maybe I should have taken a year off. I think I was quite immature when I went there.

How was your mood during that time?

I worked at a pub in Leicester, and I drank too much as a teenager. In Cambridge I was conscious of drinking too much. I don't recall feeling lonely, but I often had a sense of isolation. Alcohol seemed to help. I knew the amount I was drinking was unhealthy, but it was part of who I was at that time. The friends I'd drink with were a very important part of it. There were days when I was aware that my drinking wasn't healthy, and that it was making me do stupid things. I was getting into fights and doing crazy stuff. I got into trouble with the authorities for fighting and throwing things around, just out of control really. People provoked me, but I definitely overreacted.

Did you always have a love of writing?

Yes. I always wrote when I was growing up. I used to write songs, poems, and graphic sex stories.

How did you come to write stories for *Penthouse Forum*?

I really don't know. I've just written a novel, and in the process would sometimes say to myself, *Where do these ideas come from?* God knows. They just pop into your head. It's kind of weird.

Was it something you bragged about?

Oh, totally yes. When I first sold stories to *Penthouse Forum*, the editor said, "These are quite graphic and in the first person. Are you sure you don't want to use a pseudonym?" I said, "No way." Then she actually said, "What happens if one day you're famous and they embarrass you?" I said I wasn't worried about that. And of course when I did become well-known, it was constantly referred to.

When you finished at Cambridge, was making a career choice easy?

No, not at all. I didn't have a clue what I wanted to do. I went back on the bottle in a big way and was scraping by for a long time, working in factories. Then I applied for a training position at the *Daily Mirror*, which was extremely hard to get, and thank god I got it. I was interviewed by about ten different people. I can remember one guy, Chris Ward, having one of the *Forum* sex stories I had written on his desk. I thought, *Oh my god*, and then made a big joke about it.

Once you got into journalism, did it feel like the right career?

Yes. Fiona, who became my partner, also had a training position at the *Daily Mirror*. Fiona and I got together very quickly, and I loved being a journalist. I used to persuade myself that having a few drinks at the pub was just part of work.

What was it about journalism that ignited your spirit?

I was conscious of being a good writer. I've always been able to write incredibly quickly. I also liked the variety and the fact that everybody has a story in them. The job of the journalist, when you're living in a place called Tavistock, population eight thousand, and have a weekly paper to fill, means you have to talk to lots of people. Within two years, both Fiona and I were in Fleet Street and had jobs at national papers.

What were some of the highlights of journalism for you?

The first really big story that both Fiona and I did was the Penlee lifeboat disaster. It was rare to get a big story like that when you weren't living in a major city. It was huge—one of the biggest stories in the world at the time. During that period, somebody would tell me something in the pub, and I'd sell it to the national papers. I also did an article tracing a network of football hooligans and went to Africa to cover the famine in Ethiopia.

Was it stressful?

Yes. I was drinking a lot, which was part of the culture then. I was young and fit, so I didn't feel that stressed, but I must have been.

I understand that in 1986 you were covering Labour Opposition leader Neil Kinnock's trip to Scotland and got quite distressed. Is that right?

Yes. I basically had a complete breakdown when I was up in Scotland with Neil: I'd been drinking very heavily the day before, I was overworking, and I just felt my mind going. It felt like a complete black mess inside my head, and then I was hearing noises and music. That's when I was arrested for my own safety. They let me go, and I was hospitalized. That was my rock bottom.

That breakdown was important because it gave me a taste of my own vulnerability and mortality. It was irrational, but I seriously believed I was going to die. I was being tested—by what or whom, I didn't know—and I was failing the test, and the punishment was going to be death. This thought inspired more panic, which created more madness and greater certainty that death was only a short distance away.

Did you sense that episode approaching?

Yes. I felt it coming for quite some time. But the more people warned me about it, the more I pushed back.

Were you feeling increasing levels of anxiety or confusion?

I was actually feeling like a superman—like I could do anything I wanted. But I also had that feeling of getting more and more wired and losing things. I remember constantly losing my wallet, my jacket, and stuff like that. People were viewing me quite oddly, as well. I was very young to be such a successful journalist. I had been made an executive at twenty-eight and had people working for me. I think people thought, *Maybe this guy is sort of a creative genius—or maybe he's completely crazy*. Of course, I was probably a bit of both at the time because I was very creative and was doing quite well. But it went too far, and I think spiraling out of control was inevitable, especially given how heavily I was drinking.

How was your sleep during that period?

Bad. I was working really late, drinking really late, and getting to bed way too late. I was throwing up in the morning and going straight to work.

When you were arrested for your own safety, did you resent it?

No, I felt relieved actually. I'd been feeling more and more out of control. I felt like everything that was going [on] around me was *about* me, and I was becoming very alarmed by that. I thought I was being tested to survive. I was in the foyer of the main building of

Hamilton Council, and I started emptying my pockets on the floor and emptying my bag. Some guy said, "Are you all right?" I said, "No, I don't think I am." He said, "Maybe you should come with us," and I agreed. And I didn't even know who they were, to be honest, but I felt relieved that somebody was stepping in. When I got to the police station I took all my clothes off and was banging around, feeling the walls, and writing things on the walls.

Were there elements of psychosis?

Oh yes, totally. I was hearing voices and music. There were people singing and shouting at each other; there were conversations and all sorts of stuff going on. At one point my mind was racing and also being filled by noises—music, bagpipes, brass bands, rock bands, all clashing with each other. I stood next to an elevator, and as people walked by, I assumed they were sending me messages, whether they spoke or didn't.

And then you went to Ross Hall Hospital. You were twenty-eight and at the top of your game and suddenly in a psychiatric hospital. What was that like?

I felt an element of relief. I wrote a lot when I was there. I wrote letters I never sent. I was trying to rationalize my experience. At the height of the psychosis, I was convinced that people on television were talking just to me. It was a scary time. I know it was irrational, but I thought I was going to die. I also thought my career would be finished, but it wasn't, because my old boss took me back.

What had Fiona observed about your behavior leading up to your breakdown?

She said, "Calm down, stop drinking so much, and stop working so hard. You're being ridiculous. You're getting out of control." The more she said that, the worse I got. I kept saying to myself, *You'll be fine. Nobody else knows what they're talking about.*

What was your diagnosis and the recommended treatment?

The doctor thought I'd had a psychotic breakdown fueled by drink and overwork. He suggested I stop drinking for three months, but I ended up quitting for thirteen years. When I left the hospital I went to the West Country to stay with a friend. I didn't want to go back to London; I wanted to stay somewhere quiet. Even though I was only there for a few days, my friend says I was talking manically, still coming through it really, even though I was sedated.

And then you were back at work fairly quickly?

Yes, after a few weeks. Deciding to stop drinking was a very big thing for me. I also decided to be more open about my politics. I had persuaded myself that I was an independent journalist, but I wasn't really. I had always been very political. In addition, I decided that holidays are probably more important than I'd thought they were. So I made some changes, but I was still a workaholic. I did a BBC documentary about my breakdown, called *Cracking Up*.

I've heard that for people with an alcohol problem, going back to the same environment can be very difficult if it's a culture that promotes drinking.

I was determined. It was difficult back then because drink was always around in newsrooms. Everybody drank back then. We used to have a guy who brought a drinks trolley around in the afternoon to fill the executives' minibars. People used to steal a bottle of beer or scotch as the trolley went past, so that was the culture. Fortunately, I wasn't tempted.

Were you resolute even after a really stressful day?

Yes. I really got into it. I felt like I was achieving something, and I was very proud of that.

What made you decide to move to politics?

Circumstances and chance really. Tony Blair asked me to work for him. Would I have gone down that road otherwise? Maybe, but I hadn't actively thought of it.

Were you prepared for it? Did you fully comprehend what it involved?

Yes, I think so. I took a month to think about it, but deep down I knew I was going to do it. I really enjoyed being part of a winning team. Most of the time we were controlling the agenda, which was a nice change, but being in politics at that level is heavy and all-consuming.

How was your mood with that frenetic pace?

It was very up and down, but I hid it most of the time. I was sleeping okay, partly because I was tired. There was definitely an adrenaline thing. I ran a lot and was fitter than I'd been. Most of the time I felt that I was a round peg in a round hole and knew what I was doing. I quickly established a sense of authority in the job. Most of the politicians and the media had a certain respect for my abilities, even if the media didn't like me. I worked extremely hard, and things sometimes got difficult at home, because Fiona felt I was putting the job before the family—and you do quite often in those circumstances.

Were you ever formally diagnosed with depression?

Not then, but I was afterward. Basically, I resisted the diagnosis and was in denial. All my life I've been conscious of having low periods and drinking too much. When I eventually stepped off the political treadmill, I had a pretty big crash. A friend told me that I really ought to see somebody and recommended someone. The doctor said, "You've got classic depression and you've probably had it all your life. You can't let it go on." I saw him for a long time and ended up writing a novel, *All in the Mind,* which had a lot of depressing content. I've always written about what I was going through. If you read my diaries, you'll see that I'm often asking myself if I'm depressed.

Were you placed on medication then?

After a while I was, and I've been on different antidepressants, on and off, for the last couple of years. I had quite a bad bout a few months ago, and I've been on antidepressants for a while. I'm tapering off of them now.

What is a depressive phase like for you?

I feel less desire to connect with other people and can become antisocial to the point of reclusiveness—not answering the phone, even when friends call, and not opening mail. I find it harder to generate the enthusiasm and energy required for the strenuous physical exercise I like to do every day, and which I know is vital to my mental well-being. My curiosity and interest in the world around me, let alone a desire to try something new, vanish, and I become less giving as I become insular and isolated.

How do you feel about depression now?

I don't thank my depression and wouldn't wish it upon anyone. It is a horrible illness for which there is not enough understanding. The nearest I can come to describing it is that when it strikes, you feel dead and alive at the same time. But I'm content that I've learned to live with it, pleased that I've accepted it as part of who I am, happy that, after years of living in denial, I finally got help; and although I retain a lifelong abhorrence of drugs, pleased that I have a psychiatrist I trust enough to listen when he tells me, "I think it might be a good idea if you took a few pills for a while."

What keeps you well now? What are the foundations of your wellness?

I still have bad bouts, but certain things help: family, keeping fit, keeping busy, doing things that engage and interest me, and doing things that actually matter. Forcing myself to go out and meet people—to read about something I know nothing about or do something I've never done before can also bring immediate benefits. For example, I now do a lot of campaigning to help reduce the stigma associated with mental illness. Of all the things I do, it's probably the one that makes the least money, but it gives me the most satisfaction.

Why do you think that is?

I think a lot of people who go into politics have an inner conflict between sense of self and service to others. I struggle with that all the time. For example, I left government service in 2003, but I went back to help Tony Blair and then Gordon Brown in the general elections. It was difficult, but once I decided to do it, I was okay. I felt a pull and an obligation. I've got something similar going on now, because a lot of people are asking me to stand as a candidate, and a big part of me wants to, but another part wants me to think about myself. The thing about mental health campaigning is that it provides a sense of purpose that can turn a bad experience into something good, into an opportunity.

When I've had a driving sense of purpose, like when I was working for the Labour Party and the Labour government, it felt right. I didn't like what the conservatives did to Britain, and I was in a position where I could do something about that, which felt really good. People often asked if I was happy doing the job. A lot of the time, no, but I am happy that I did it.

My breakdown was one of the worst things that has happened to me on one level, but it was also one of the most extraordinary experiences of my life. It's led me to write novels, get involved in issues at a deeper level, and hopefully help other people and change attitudes. Although it was bad, some good came of it. This sort of clash between self and service is always going to be a thing with me. When I talk to my psychiatrist about my depression, he seems to think that's where it's coming from. You want to be free and do your own thing, to put yourself first, but you feel strong pressures not to do that.

A couple of very successful political leaders, such as Abraham Lincoln and Winston Churchill, had mental illnesses. Do you think that someone with a mental illness could win the highest office in today's political system?

I think it would be very hard—much harder than it was back then. There was a debate in the House of Commons where four members of parliament spoke out about their struggles with depression, and they got a very good reception.

Lincoln is commonly described as the greatest American president ever. Churchill is commonly described as the greatest British prime minister ever. Yet even with Churchill's obvious competence, I can't see that, in today's twenty-four-hour news cycle, the press or public would tolerate him having one of those days when he couldn't get out of bed until two in the afternoon. I can just see a reporter outside 10 Downing Street in a live report saying, "We've heard that the prime minister is still not up. We'll take the weather, and then we'll go back and find out if he's out of bed yet."

Lincoln had really profound bouts of melancholia. I think the workload of modern leaders has been increased because of the Internet and a relentless media. It's very unforgiving. I think it could be very difficult.

I know I'm not in the Lincoln or Churchill league, but even though I've gotten a lot of unfair press, their accounts of my struggles with depression have actually been pretty good.

When I list good things and bad things in my life, one of the good things I put down is that I have been open about having mental health problems and get a very positive response from that. I get people stopping me every day, saying they have a brother, sister, dad, or mum struggling with a mental health issue, or that they are. They tell me how helpful it is that somebody with a high profile talks about it the way that I do.

If people have been through difficult times, I think they have more empathy. The other thing I see about my breakdown is that it's given me a yardstick for thinking about how I feel and how other people feel. So if I'm going through a crisis, one of the first things I would say to myself is, *Is this really a crisis?* To me, a crisis is when you're kind of on the edge. In government, it's like your government's about to go under. For a country, it's like the economy's crashing or the country is on the verge of war. These are crises. I often think my breakdown helped me say to people, "Look, this is bad, but it's not a crisis for Christ's sake. Let's just carry on and not worry too much." I think people who have endured hard times, be it mental illness, grief, or physical illness, are better equipped to do that.

If you could go back and give your eighteen-year-old self advice, what would you say?

Don't drink so much. When my father dropped me off at university, he gave me a quote from *Hamlet*: "To thine own self be true." It's the same advice I would give my own three children. They don't teach that in school, and it isn't easy to work out what that means, but life will tell you eventually. I'd probably advise myself to be more tolerant of people who disagree or are different. But then again, part of what allowed me to do the job I did successfully was that I was a control freak. At that time, in that job, that was necessary.

When I think of the really big things in my life, I'm so grateful for Fiona—who[m] I've been with for thirty-three years, and hopefully will be for a lot longer—the kids, my parents, my football, and the extraordinary plethora of experiences I've had. In a way, I had them because I've always taken risks and wanted to do things that most people don't do. Even at a young age, I felt I was different, a bit special, and did things most people don't do. Once, when I was a teenager living in Leicester, during the Ashes, a cricket series between England and Australia, I heard that the Australian players were having a few drinks at the local golf club. I said to myself, *I'm going to get into that*, and I did. I ended up at the bar joking with Rodney Marsh, a famous Australian player at the time.

It drives Fiona crazy, but I constantly tell her I don't think I've done enough in my life. I need to do more. I need new challenges. And she'll say, "For God's sake, you've done more than most people are ever going to do. Just chill out." But I find it quite difficult to do that.

WHAT WORKS FOR ALASTAIR

- Giving up alcohol
- Writing about his experiences
- Exercising
- Receiving support from family and friends
- Finding the right medication
- Finding purpose in work
- Gaining a sense of well-being from mental health advocacy

CHAPTER 5

LORA INMAN

A Journey from Depression to Mental Health Advocacy

ORIGINALLY FROM CALIFORNIA, LORA INMAN HAS lived in many states across the United States, from the Pacific Northwest to the east coast of Florida. She fought a lengthy battle against major depression, which greatly impacted her career and personal life and contributed to three broken marriages. Throughout her struggle, she's done extensive research on mood disorders, motivated by a strong determination to understand depression, and with the goal of finding a way to live and even thrive in the face of this life-altering illness. She has now been in remission for over nine years.

As a longtime member of the National Alliance on Mental Illness (NAMI) and the Depression and Bipolar Support Alliance (DBSA), Lora has stayed up-to-date on new treatments for depression and bipolar disorder. As an advocate for mental health, she has spoken on major depression and bipolar disorder to groups in

Jacksonville, Florida, and in the Chicago area. She currently serves as secretary of the board of directors for NAMI Jacksonville.

Lora wrote a memoir about her journey through major depression, titled *Running Uphill* (2008). The feedback she's received, and the knowledge that others have benefited from her difficult experiences, is immensely meaningful to her.

Lora, could you tell me a bit about your childhood?

My childhood was quite dysfunctional. My mother and father were divorced when I was very young. I don't remember my father ever being around. My mother was quite a religious fanatic, to the extent that she didn't believe in illness, much less treating it. When I was younger, I believe I was dysphoric most of the time. Dysphoria is essentially a less severe but ongoing form of depression. I lived with that from about age eleven throughout my teenage years.

Were you an only child?

I wasn't. My mother remarried, and I had a half sister who was six years younger. She ultimately took her own life at age forty-five, leaving behind a young son who was greatly impacted by the death of his mother.

When you say your mother was very religious, what impact did that have on you?

It had a huge impact. For one thing, I never saw a doctor, and for another, my sister and I didn't get vaccinations like other kids did. If I was sick, had a headache, or was sick to my stomach, my mother's belief was that if you denied it strongly enough, it simply didn't exist. At age seventeen I discovered that I had some kind of growth in my stomach, but we didn't go to doctors—we just prayed about it. When I got married at seventeen, I went to a doctor for the first time and discovered I had a nineteen-pound ovarian cyst that I'd been carrying around for six or seven years. This disfiguration greatly affected my self-esteem throughout high school because I didn't have the body my peers had, and felt like an anomaly.

Was your stepfather also very religious?

No, he wasn't. I never felt love in my family. Nobody ever seemed to be happy and joyous, and our home was always cold and quiet. My mother didn't allow me to play the popular music that the teenagers were listening to because she would be busy studying her religious literature, so I felt quite ostracized and in the dark about what other kids my age were experiencing.

Did your mother expect you to be as fanatical about religion as she was?

Absolutely. When I left home and had surgery for the ovarian cyst, she was very angry at me. She told my cousin that it was my own fault for believing a lie. She said it was my fault for having the surgery and seeming to have that nineteen-pound ovarian cyst. It was my fault because I didn't pray and believe enough.

What led you to get married at seventeen?

I wanted to get away from my extremely dysfunctional family. And there was a man I'd dated through high school who purported to love me. I didn't think anybody else ever would. But the marriage was very abusive. I remember him slapping me across the face and locking me in a closet one day and then taking off in the car. It wasn't a nurturing marriage. I found out later that he'd been unfaithful to me many, many times. We were only married four years.

How was your mood during that time?

Through my first marriage I wasn't clinically depressed, but I wasn't happy. I got by on a low level of functioning. When my husband was drafted for the Vietnam War, I realized that I really could take care of myself and didn't have to put up with that kind of abuse. I filed for divorce when he was in Vietnam, and he got an emergency leave to come home and finalize it. At least I got him out of Vietnam. He didn't have to return.

You were divorced at twenty-one. What happened next?

Once I realized that I was capable of supporting myself, I got a job and a roommate, and life was okay. My mood was okay for quite a while, but then I started having minor episodes of depression.

What brought those on?

I really can't tell you anything that brought it on. That's how my depressions have been. They never seemed to be preceded by something else. Life could just be sailing along, with everything going great, and then it was like a black cloud just dumped on me. Instantly, overnight, I would wake up with a horrible sense of foreboding, fear, aloneness, and terror.

The first really severe episode of major depression I had occurred when I was working for a company in Kansas. The company was moving its headquarters to Arizona, and I was asked to move with them. When I first arrived in Arizona, I realized that change can bring on depression because it's so stressful. About the second week I was there, my first episode of real major depression hit me. I could barely function. I had a complete sense of isolation and felt I just didn't fit in with the rest of the world.

Were you able to talk to anyone about it, such as a friend or a doctor?

Absolutely not. I tried to find somebody to talk to, but when I'd say I was feeling really depressed, people backed off. Nobody wanted to hear about it. I thought I was crazy because I didn't know anybody else who had these kinds of feelings. I thought I was an anomaly.

When did that first major episode start to lift?

The amazing thing is, the depression would come out of nowhere and last for approximately ten days. You could count it: ten days and then it would go away. Then I would be okay for a while, until another episode hit. There was precious little information out there in the late 1960s and early 1970s. I finally went to a psychiatrist, but he was of little use. He didn't seem to consider the possibility of a chemical imbalance or anything like that.

Later on, I did a lot of research on my own to try to find out what was wrong with me and if other people had similar problems. I called doctors, wrote letters, and did everything I could. Back then, you couldn't just Google "depression," and there were no ads for antidepressants on TV. I felt so alone. I even went to see a doctor in another state because I wanted to find out why this was happening. By then, I knew that I didn't fit the standard definition of major depression because the episodes only lasted ten days, not the fourteen days required for an official diagnosis.

What happened next?

I had gotten married again, this time to a pilot. My second husband is the father of my son, Darin. He traveled a great deal with his job and developed a really negative attitude after the birth of our son, which caused a lot of problems in our marriage. I went through some major postpartum depression, and he didn't understand what was wrong with me. He had no knowledge of major depression. The marriage eventually ended in divorce after four years.

Did anyone diagnose postpartum depression?

For the first time in my life, someone diagnosed what had caused me so many problems. My ob-gyn pronounced that I had depression, in this case postpartum depression. I know a lot of women have this, and for many it's a temporary thing, but for me it was extremely severe. The hopelessness and despair and the feeling that I was alone were overwhelming. Unlike my previous episodes of depression, this went on for much longer than ten days. But again, it left mysteriously.

Being a single mom, how did you support yourself financially?

I worked with one company for eight years and made enough money to support Darin and myself. I had some episodes of depression after the divorce, but for the most part, I functioned okay. I didn't always feel like working, but I forced myself to because I had no choice. I couldn't allow Darin to be affected by my moods. Fortunately, throughout this period of being single I didn't have any severe episodes of depression. It was milder and easier to get through. It didn't have a great effect on Darin, and that was my main concern.

And then what happened?

Believe it or not, after about four years I got married again, this time to someone that I met through my work. My job was to train people to run high-volume copiers, so I often went out to client sites. That's how I met my last husband. We had only known each other two months when he asked me to marry him. It was nuts, because we had absolutely nothing in common. Plus, he was very unemotional, whereas I felt like the most emotional person walking the planet.

How was your mood during that period?

Up and down. I'd have ten to twelve days of severe depression, followed by periods of normalcy. I wasn't bipolar; I didn't have mania. Between episodes, I was just what I would call normal. Every time I went into a depression, I'd think, *I'm never going to feel good again. I'm not going to make it through this. I can't handle this kind of pain.* I remember saying things to my husband like "If something should happen to me, please promise you'll take care of Darin." I never had a suicide plan or attempted suicide, but I did entertain thoughts of ending my life because it was too painful to be alive.

When you were going through those really tough times, were you able to work?

I was, which was amazing. I was a great actress, and when I had to, I could pull it together. There were times when my depression was too severe, but for the most part I was able to put on the mask.

I was desperate for approval, especially when I was depressed. When I wasn't depressed, my self-esteem was quite good. I went to college, took some classes, and ended up getting my associate degree. I functioned quite well, but the depression still came and went.

And your marriage?

I found out my third husband was unfaithful, and we ended up getting a divorce. So, there I was in singledom again. I moved back with my son to Seattle. As soon as we arrived in Seattle, I had a nervous breakdown. I literally could not function. I would get up every morning, as it was an agitated depression; I'd have to get out of bed. I took a shower every single day, and then I would either just sit or get in my car, drive around, and park somewhere. I needed to see people actually walking and talking. I could sit there in my parked car for an entire day, just watching.

Did you try medication at all during that period?

I had been put on medication after Darin's birth, and I'd felt a huge sense of relief that finally somebody was trying to do something to fix me. Over the years I've tried numerous medications.

I was finally put on monoamine oxidase inhibitors, or MAOIs, a type of antidepressant. For a while, I actually thought they'd found the magic pill. The pain lifted suddenly, and I had a couple of years without a major depressive episode. I thought I'd found my magic cure. I even wrote a paper about it when I was back in college. Unfortunately, that didn't last, and I crashed again. After trying a few more medications, in desperation I went to an exorcist, because I thought, *Maybe I'm possessed.* There was nothing I wouldn't try to get better—nothing. Eventually I tried electroconvulsive therapy, or shock therapy, and had a total of twenty-nine treatments. Surprisingly, this led to hypomania, which is an elevated mood.

Why did you decide to undergo electroconvulsive therapy, or ECT? Was it just desperation?

Yes. It seemed like there was nothing left to try except ECT. I felt I had tried every drug on the market. I tried all sorts of things that people said could cure depression in five days. There was nothing I didn't try, and nothing worked long term, so it was my last resort.

How did the ECT treatments affect you?

After my very first ECT session, I remember feeling as though I couldn't control myself or my thoughts. It was a scary, scary thing. It was not a good experience. There are two types of ECT, either unilateral or bilateral. They did mine bilaterally, which means the electrodes are placed on both temples instead of just one. A lot of psychiatrists say that bilateral ECT is more effective, but it also causes more memory loss and confusion, which I definitely experienced.

But some days I would wake up and the depression would be gone. It was like I was healed and had this incredible energy. Life was wonderful, and I could do anything. I was going to write a famous book. It was a feeling of complete elation, but not the mania I've seen in some people, who spend thousands of dollars, go out and have sex with countless people, or get to where they think they can walk on air. I never was at that manic point; it was simply hypomania, which is literally mild mania.

Whenever anybody asks me what I think about ECT, I say, "When you get to that point where you don't think there's any other reason to keep on living, try ECT. After all, what have you got to lose?" It did bring me out of a severe depression, but it didn't cure me. I always relapsed eventually.

When did you feel you started to get things under control?

About ten years ago, when I was living in Chicago, I found a woman psychiatrist who I credit with saving my life. She told me that she would stick with me until we found something that worked, and I believed her. I think hope is the most important thing any psychiatrist can offer their patients. I encountered a lot of doctors who didn't offer me hope, and if you don't have hope, you may as well throw it in. After meeting with her, I had a couple of ECT treatments. She didn't administer them, but she came to the hospital to see me when I had them. That's the kind of doctor she was.

It's now been over nine years since I had an episode of major depression. When people ask me what made the difference, I credit finally finding the right medication and working with a doctor I trusted—and one who made me believe I could get better. My faith in God also allowed me to hang in there. It's not an exact science, but that's how I feel.

How many medications did you try with the psychiatrist in Seattle?

Probably four or five different medications, sometimes in combination.

It sounds like the emotional support and hope that psychiatrist provided was just as important as the medication.

Absolutely. I remember walking into her office in tears and deeply depressed. She offered reassurance and was very compassionate. I remember going to a previous psychiatrist crying, and he told me that there wasn't a cure for depression. More than anything else, you've got to have a doctor who will let you believe, even if it's not true, that you're going to get better.

Beyond medication, what else has been helpful?

After my recovery, I facilitated support groups and counseled others. The nice thing about counseling peers is that they see you've survived, so they say to themselves, *Wow! If she can survive, so can I.* Those of us who have actually lived with a mood disorder or mental illness have deep credibility when we tell others that they can get through it.

I've gone into inpatient hospital settings and had people's absolute attention, because they're thinking, *Wow! You've been there? You've had that many shock treatments? Oh my god, look at you.* I get an immeasurable amount of gratification from just knowing that I've given somebody hope. I would have given anything to have that when I was going through depression.

Are there any other lifestyle strategies that help with your mental health?

Well, I've always known that exercise is good for me, but I don't always find it easy to get out there. Eating healthily is also good, as is spending time outside. It all helps. My faith in God has been essential.

Your faith is really important to you. I'm intrigued by that because you grew up with your mother's extreme version of religion, and it sounds like you have a very different philosophy now.

My mother and I never saw eye to eye regarding her religious beliefs. Even after I left home, she continued to try to persuade me to come to her line of thinking, but I never did. As I began to understand how much she had suffered and how she herself had been brainwashed by her own mother, I felt a deep sorrow for her. By the end of her life, I think I was a great comfort to her. As crazy as I thought some of her beliefs were, I loved her, and I know she loved me and was very proud of me.

My own opinion is that everybody's entitled to believe in what they want to. The reason I didn't talk much about my faith in this interview or in my book, *Running Uphill,* is that a lot of people are turned off by religion. I was one of them, so I try to inject just a little bit of faith when I give people advice. I don't believe that God comes down, magically lays his hands on you, and suddenly you're healed and walk away. That's just not my feeling. But I do know that there is a power out there that's greater than me, and it helps me get through life.

Looking back now, do you see any benefits of what you went through?

I do. It's not something that I'd want to go through again, believe me, but it has made me a more compassionate person. It's also made me a more grateful and less judgmental person. It's made me a better person in a lot of ways.

You started writing your book, *Running Uphill,* in 2007. Was that cathartic for you? And what kind of feedback did you receive from readers?

It was very cathartic for me. It was also a little painful at times because I had to relive certain things. It wasn't a great seller right away because I wasn't really involved in mental health advocacy as much as I am now. Since I started working with support groups in the last few years, I've had doctors and patients read my book, and they've said it's the best book they've ever read about depression. They said they knew exactly what I was talking about. When I first wrote it, I told myself, *If this helps one person, then it's worth it.* I haven't made any money from the book, but it's been extremely gratifying to feel that I've helped others by discussing my demons.

What gives you pleasure now?

Many, many things—things that I think give most people pleasure when they don't have to deal with an illness like major depression: spending time with friends, traveling, and doing things outdoors. I still enjoy working with people, and I plan to find employment again, this time working with people with mood disorders. I get a lot of pleasure out of life, which I never was able to experience when I was going through depression.

If, knowing what you know now, you could give your seventeen-year-old self advice, what would that be?

I think it's so important that people get a correct diagnosis, because that's the key to the right treatment. I also would have been much more persistent about finding a doctor who cared. In my earlier years, I accepted the doctors that came my way. If I could do it over again, I would first and foremost make sure my doctors cared.

I got married at seventeen because I wanted to leave a very dysfunctional family life, so I'm not sure I would have done that differently. It was the lesser of two evils. But I definitely would have made different choices in husbands if I had my time again. In marriage, it's essential that both people feel they can be open and honest with each other without getting an overly critical or negative response. So I'd also ask myself, *Is this person flexible or very opinionated?* I would avoid control freaks and look at the quality of the other person's family relationships. The most important quality is how they treat other people. That says a lot about a person.

Is there anything else you'd like to share?

I did marry a fourth time, to my husband of eighteen years. He has been very supportive and made a huge effort to understand the illness. It's imperative that your spouse or significant other learns to understand the disease; it makes the struggle so much easier to bear. Also, when you're a parent, I think the most horrid thing in the world you can do to your child is to take your life. I've had treatment-resistant depression and I've had suicidal thoughts. There were many times when I didn't think I could live one more day. And I am so incredibly glad that I did live one more day, because it's worth it. My best advice is *never give up*! It truly is possible to get better and learn not only to survive, but to actually enjoy living again.

WHAT WORKS FOR LORA

- Working with a psychiatrist who truly cares
- Finding the right medication
- Helping others with mood disorders
- Wanting to be well for her son
- Exercising and getting outside
- Eating healthily

CHAPTER 6

BOB BOORSTIN

Director, Public Policy at Google

BOB BOORSTIN IS CURRENTLY DIRECTOR OF public policy in the Washington, DC, office of Google Inc. Over the past twenty-five years, Bob has worked in national security, political communications, research, and journalism. He served for more than seven years with the Clinton administration, acting as the president's national security speechwriter. He was also communications and foreign policy advisor to Treasury Secretary Robert Rubin and advisor on the developing world to Secretary of State Warren Christopher.

He has worked on more than a dozen national and international political campaigns, and has advised Fortune 500 CEOs and some of the nation's leading advocacy groups. Prior to working at Google, he helped found the Center for American Progress, a progressive public policy research and advocacy group, and served as its senior vice president for national security.

Early in his career, Boorstin was a reporter for the *New York Times*. A graduate of Harvard University in 1981, he received a master's degree in international relations from King's College, Cambridge University, in 1983.

He had a happy childhood until his father died suddenly when he was nine years old, but he considers himself lucky because, as he says, he "won the stepparent lottery" when Alan Pakula, film director, producer, and writer, came into his life.

Despite Bob's extraordinary career success, he has struggled with bipolar disorder since his diagnosis at age twenty-seven. He's learned a number of strategies to manage his illness and finds immense satisfaction in advocating on behalf of those living with mental illness.

Bob, can you tell me a bit about your childhood?

I was born in 1959 in Dallas, Texas, but I grew up in Beverly Hills, California. I guess you could say I had a normal childhood, if there is such a thing in an incredibly wealthy place like Beverly Hills. I have a fraternal twin brother—I'm forty-five minutes older—and I have a sister who's about two years older. As it turns out, my brother escaped bipolar disorder, and my sister has lived with depression.

When you look back, do you consider your childhood happy?

Absolutely. We were well provided for, to say the least. I think there were two things that were disturbing in my childhood. One was having a tendency toward perfectionism, which often left me frustrated. I cried a great deal as a kid, and when I look back on that now, I see it as kind of a warning sign for what came later.

Then, when I was nine, my father died suddenly of a heart attack. That clearly had wide implications for our family, my character, and my psyche.

How did the family change?

Unlike most families, we didn't have to move, and our material circumstances didn't change that much. But it certainly affected me as a child. I became more morose. Let me put it this way: when the message of the graduation speaker at my high school was "Life isn't fair," I had already figured that out.

I think a couple of things about my father's death influenced me in important ways later in life. One was that I didn't know my dad was sick before he died. Several years later when my mother told me, I became incensed. I think that had a lot to do with my later decision to be open about my own illness and to share the details of my illness with my kids.

I think his death also caused me to want to be like the "white knight" character in life: a guy who comes rushing in and is there to rescue people. As ridiculous as it sounds, when you're nine years old and lose your father, even if you're only forty-five minutes older than your twin, you do assume this kind of "man of the house" thing. That can put a lot of undue pressure on a child—not intentionally by someone else, but simply self-inflicted. I think many depressives spend a lot of life putting pressure on themselves and then being unable to live up to their expectations. I certainly established that pattern when I was young.

What sort of things did you feel you had to do as the head of the house?

More than anything else, protect my mom. One of the ways I did that was by never going through the typical teenage rebellion.

Somewhere in the back of the mind of every child who loses a parent at a young age is a feeling that you actually killed that parent. Anybody who is honest and has gone through this would tell you that. After it happens, I think there's a tendency to dial back the rage and rebellion of the teenage years so you don't end up somehow killing the parent who's still alive.

At the same time, I'm lucky because my mother remarried when I was thirteen. She married Alan [film director and writer Alan Pakula], and he proved to be my best friend until he died suddenly. As sad as the circumstances of my father's death were, I was lucky because I had my stepfather in my life for more than twenty years. How many people get two good fathers? How many people get even one good father?

What was so special about your stepfather?

I was drawn to him at first because of what he did. When I was a kid, I did nothing but make little films for class, from the age of eight to thirteen. I stopped when he came into the family, of course. That was the first thing that I admired about him: what he did and how well he did it.

But far beyond that, there was a warmth, [an] understanding and undemanding way about him that I simply can't describe with any justice. I'll give you an example. When I went to prep school in Connecticut, I wasn't in great shape. I was getting physically beaten up, and it was an unpleasant time. One day I talked to my parents on the phone about how I was doing, and my stepfather heard something in my voice. The next day he showed up. He flew cross-country just to have dinner with me and to make sure I was okay.

You mentioned that you were prone to perfectionist tendencies as a child. How did that manifest itself?

In school assignments, I wasn't satisfied unless everything was perfect. I literally cried over tiny things that went wrong. I always wanted to have control of the situation, and I think that's often a sign of perfectionism.

You said you were bullied at school. What impact did that have on you?

I think it made me more obnoxious and aggressive. Obviously, it was also humiliating. The one thing I'd say about it, and similar to the impact of my illness, is that it made me more understanding of other people's faults and frailties. I'm less quick to judge.

You went to Harvard to study to be a geneticist and didn't enjoy it, and then found a real interest in modern Chinese history. Did that have to do with all the writers in your family, including your mother and uncle, the historian Daniel Boorstin?

A little. To be honest, my uncle and my father, who was thirteen years his junior, were not close. My uncle was basically disinherited from the family when he married my aunt. I was the first child on my father's side to really get to know my uncle. I had an internship with a senator in Washington [D. C.] when I was a junior in high school. My uncle had just taken over the Library of Congress and was living in Washington, and I spent some time with him. I'm fairly sure he had elements of manic depression, just never treated. He would get up at four in the morning and write for four hours before going to his day job. He wrote big books. His books make these extraordinary connections between historical events. He found patterns in history in a way that not many historians do. Finding the connective tissue and connections in history is something that many, many manic-depressives do.

When do you think you had your first manic episode?

When I was twenty-seven. It had a lot to do with the fact that I grew late. When I went to college at seventeen, I was only four foot eleven. I tend to link the onset of depression and manic depression to the age that people go through puberty and grow. I also think part of the reason my onset was so late was that I was able to control my hypomania, for the most part, during my twenties.

Was there a pattern that led to your first episode?

Yes. I remember one instance in particular. I had been working at the *New York Times* for about two years when two things happened to me. The first was that I was sent to Houston to write an obituary of one of the astronauts who died in the space shuttle *Challenger* explosion. I was already in a deep depression. It was the dead of winter in New York. It was snowing, it was dark, and I was miserable. I was on the night shift. I hadn't been diagnosed, and I just felt like I was dying.

Then they decided to send me off to write that obituary. I went down to Houston, where at least the weather was nicer, but I couldn't get word one from the family about the astronaut, which I understood. After all, they'd just lost their father and husband. Also, the family was Japanese, who tend to be particularly private about these things. I couldn't write the story. I just sat there, chewed my fingers away, and couldn't get anything done.

I finally turned in the story and went back to New York. I remember being so scared of walking into the newsroom that I claimed to be sick for a couple of days. I got up the nerve to go see my shrink, who I was seeing four times a week in psychotherapy, almost psychoanalysis really. I screamed and wept and wailed for an hour.

Later I had a better shrink, and when we talked about that time, he said, "This wasn't an easy story for you to write. After all, it was a story of a father who went up into the air and never came back, just like your dad." My father had been on vacation in Europe with my mother when he died, and he never came back. I didn't realize the psychological significance of that.

So that was the first terrible thing that happened to me. At the same time, as mentioned, I was on the night shift, which is terrible for anybody who has manic depression. You never see the sunlight, and you have no social life. Then, at the end of March, I went on a pilgrimage of sorts with my girlfriend to see the place in Greece where my father had died. We first went to Athens, and then to Rhodes, where my father had died under the statue of the Colossus.

I thought that going there and seeing the place where he died would be a very important moment for me, but I didn't feel anything. All I felt was some disappointment that the trip wasn't going well with my girlfriend and we were fighting about this and that. At the end of May, we broke up. I remember the moment vividly. I was literally beating my legs with my hands while talking with her.

Wisely, she'd had enough of me. I didn't realize what was actually wrong. If I had, I would have done something about it. My shrink had never said, "You might have biological depression." Then, as summer arrived, my mood shifted completely and I became hyperactive and hypomanic. I started to write two or three articles in a day for the *New York Times*.

I became quite glib, the way that people do when they're manic. All sorts of things happened that made me more active than normal, moving quickly and becoming more liberal with money. I became more sexually aggressive. I had a couple of girlfriends at that time. For the first time in my life, I made very fast and obvious passes and succeeded.

The first bipolar episode happened when I hadn't slept for about a week. I was down in Washington and did a panel discussion. I spent the night at a friend's house and couldn't sleep, then went to the *New York Times* office in Washington the next day. Something in the back of my mind said, *There's something wrong.* I didn't know what it was, but it caused me to call my stepfather's assistant and ask for help.

My stepfather and my mother flew down from New York and took me back to the city. But first I made them stop at the Jefferson Memorial, and while we were there I told them the history of the world according to me, as people who are in the midst of delusional episodes tend to do. On the flight back to New York, I thought I was in control of the plane. My parents took me to my doctor, who said, "You have to hospitalize him. He's clearly having a manic episode." My parents took me down to Payne Whitney in New York, where I was hospitalized.

What do you recall from that time?

I think one's recollection of such times is never clear. I recall being drugged heavily with antipsychotics. I always say that antipsychotics are like steel wool. When you burn something in a pan, you have to use them to get out the remains.

I do recall outrageous behavior, like running naked through the halls of the mental hospital. I also remember being put into what's called a quiet room, which has a mattress and a window and nothing else. I thought I could fly and tried to climb out the window, but was held back by the fact that windows in mental hospitals don't open more than a few inches.

I remember sessions with doctors, trying to talk to them about what it felt [like] to be high. I remember a lot of my friends visiting. I certainly remember trying to leave the place immediately and being subject to a forty-eight-hour rule. You could apply to get out, but you had to wait until forty-eight hours after you made the application to leave.

I remember a slow regaining of sanity, of ideas and purposes and life returning to normal. I remember feeling humiliated and embarrassed but also pleased and relieved that I finally had something to point at—something that had caused all of my crying, misery, depression, and odd behavior over the years.

That something had a name: manic depression. I had a diagnosis. I remember being quite angry with my shrink at the time, because he had never suggested that I could have a biological illness. I thought that he had blown it completely.

What happened after that?

I had already planned to move to Boston because I'd had an unhappy time in my job at the *New York Times*. I moved to Boston to work on the presidential campaign of Michael Dukakis, who I had known when I was an undergraduate at Harvard. A couple of people I knew well from the Kennedy School at Harvard were running his campaign, and they asked me to come work on the campaign with them.

Ideologically, it was a good fit for me, so I moved up to Boston, but only after I made guarantees that I would see a doctor at least once a week and make sure to take my medication.

Did you feel comfortable sharing what you had been through with anyone other than your immediate family?

Yeah. I shared it with a lot of my friends. It was hard, but I told them about things like when I tried to jump out a window thinking I could fly. I didn't feel comfortable enough to tell them about running down the halls naked.

My case is unusual for a number of reasons. First, I have a garden-variety case of manic depression. By that, I mean I respond well to most drugs, to treatment, and to talk therapy in general. Second, I came from a family that's very open and tolerant. They were scared, but they were able to absorb the fact that I had an illness. Too often, the family goes into complete denial for either cultural or personal reasons.

Third, and frankly, my parents were wealthy enough that they could afford to help me with health care. Fourth, my parents were extraordinarily tolerant and well-read, and because they had encountered these kinds of illnesses previously, the implications weren't lost on them. Many years earlier, my stepfather had produced a film called *Fear Strikes Out*, about Jimmy Piersall, an outfielder for the Boston Red Sox. The movie is all about the relationship between Jimmy, played by Anthony Perkins, who is slowly going mad, and his father, played by Karl Malden, who tries to convince him that there's nothing wrong.

When you went to the Dukakis campaign, were people aware of your episode?

Yes. I told them because I didn't want to take anybody by surprise if it happened again. Telling them was self-protective on two fronts:

one, I didn't want to end up in a bad place, and two, I didn't want to lose my job.

I started seeing an excellent doctor just outside of Boston. We worked through some of the emotional issues attached to being diagnosed, and I slowly began to move from the stage of "I am the illness" to "I have this illness."

Things with Dukakis heated up, obviously. I worked in a lot of places. In Pennsylvania, I got hypomanic as I worked to get a bunch of different leaflets together because of the way the voting system works there. I ended up staying up late and not being able to sleep well, and I couldn't really feel the episode coming on.

We went on to New York State, and I suddenly started acting more glib and garrulous. I started having the same kind of behavior as before, spending more money and making more bullish comments about the prospects of our campaign in the absence of real evidence. I had a bad time the night of the primary. I drank excessively, and I was making a play for a woman who clearly wasn't interested, but I couldn't see that.

The day after the New York primary we went back to Boston, and I was high as a kite. I went into an electronics store and bought thousands and thousands of dollars' worth of equipment, thinking I was going to load it all into my car and drive to wherever they were going to assign me next. Over the course of that day, it became increasingly clear to me that I needed the equipment because I was being monitored and watched.

In the early afternoon, I went to the hotel across the street from the campaign headquarters, the Lafayette Hotel, and somehow managed to sneak my way into the presidential suite. I had a typical delusion where the hotel suddenly turned into the starship *Enterprise*, which was about to take off, and I was the captain in charge of it. At that point, the police came in.

I was taken to the nearest hospital: Massachusetts General. I was strapped down to a gurney and raving. Two things happened that were lucky. The first was that the emergency room doctor who examined me turned out to be a classmate of mine from elementary school, who[m] I hadn't seen in thirty years. The second thing was that they found my campaign ID, called, and got my assistant, who I'd told about my illness. I had given her my shrink's number and told her, "If you ever get a call that says that I'm doing something really strange, I want you to call this person and get him to me." She called him immediately.

My shrink came running from Newton. He had me sent out to McLean Hospital outside Boston, which is kind of the Ritz-Carlton of mental hospitals. As it turned out, my episode apparently arose not from anything natural, but because I was on too high a dose of desipramine, an antidepressant. Then the hospital said my insurance wouldn't cover my stay, so they couldn't admit me. My brother, who was the emergency contact I listed, had to guarantee eighteen thousand dollars on his American Express card in order to get me into the hospital.

When I came out of the hospital several weeks later and learned about them refusing to admit me, it started a lifetime of commitment to mental health activism. I also got very angry. One of the ways that I expressed my anger was hiring a law firm to represent me against my insurance company, which had refused to pay for my hospitalization. I eventually won a settlement.

Did you start to get some insight into the medication and other things that helped you?

Yeah. I had already realized that the right medication in the right dose was important. I started to realize that going to therapy was also important.

Then I discovered the value of support groups. My shrink insisted I go, and I quickly learned that support groups are valuable because they remind you that you aren't alone. I remember vividly the first time I went. After being asked to introduce myself, I said, "I'm Bob and I had this episode." Somebody said, "What was the episode like?" I told them about the starship *Enterprise* episode and thinking I was Christ, and they just sat there nodding like it was normal. It was reassuring in the most bizarre way.

You had some bad depressive episodes after that initial time. What brought them on?

Two things bring them on for me. One is what psychiatrists call "life events," and the second is winter. In the late fall, I usually end up in a pretty bad way. I have to take more antidepressants, and I have to sit in front of my light box. If I'm lucky, I come out of it quickly. This year, I went through an awful two-month episode that left me in bed for days at a time, unable to do anything.

When you were in politics, working very long hours and sometimes going without sleep, how did you handle it?

I didn't always succeed. I think the people who are more successful in handling this illness are their own best guarantors. They've studied their own patterns. I always tell people who are considering going into therapy or who are already in counseling that the point of therapy is to become your own therapist.

I think self-awareness and monitoring oneself are really important. Another thing I did was make sure the alarm bells would go off when needed. I made a deal with my mom that she was to call my shrink if she heard anything in my voice that worried her. I'd recommend that strategy to almost anybody: give someone they trust permission to talk to the shrink in case something goes haywire.

That's an excellent idea, because often people can't recognize it in themselves.

No, of course not. That's true in depression, and even more so in mania. Sometimes you lose it and become a total pain in the ass to your family and friends. There ought to be one of them who has permission to call the shrink and say, "Hey, Bob is acting up. Bob is high," or "Bob seems very low. We ought to do something about this."

Coping with stress is extremely hard. One thing I do almost religiously in the worst stressful times is exercise. I find that it's important not just in keeping depression at bay, but also in keeping me calm.

Another thing I've done over the years is nap regularly. When I was in the White House, I made them move a couch into my office, and in the afternoon I'd take an hour-long nap.

I also took vacations, which people who were my age in government rarely did. They had this bizarre thought that if they were to leave and go on vacation, the government would grind to a halt. I never really adopted that feeling, and more importantly, I knew that if I didn't take a vacation, I'd self-destruct.

Are there warning signs that you can recognize in yourself?

Oh my god, yes. There are two sets. For getting depressed, the first warning sign is the need for more sleep and an inability to get out of bed. Another sign is eating more or not at all. The change in eating pattern is always an important sign for me. Another is stopping exercise or losing interest in anything that's good for me. That's a major problem.

Another sign of depression is emotional reaction to things that normally wouldn't disturb me, like television commercials. When I'm down, *Finding Nemo* makes me cry. I see it not as the fun cartoon but as the story of a father letting go of his son. Lower sex drive is also a sign. At the worst, I had thoughts of suicide or self-destructive behavior, which are obvious warning signs. For example, I've thought about what it would be like for my kids if I was gone. That's when I know I am in really deep shit.

For manic times, glib and garrulous behavior is number one for me. When I start talking too much, sharing too much, and being too honest with people, it's not good. I also get hypersexual, which is a clear sign that I'm heading up. Another sign is that I start to break little rules that I use to keep me in check.

When you were in the White House, were you able to do any advocacy?

Absolutely. When I was on the Clinton campaign in 1992, I claimed the mental health portfolio. Clinton was fine with it. My first job in the White House was to work as the communications person for Hillary Clinton on the health care reform campaign.

I was also allowed to participate in the health care task force and help bring together people in the government and outside the government in the fight for mental health legislation. I helped bring together outside lobbying groups that care about mental health issues into an alliance of sorts that lobbied successfully. I also had the opportunity to help break out some extraordinary data from the Veterans Administration on veterans and their incidence of mental health problems.

All through my time in government, mental health was something I paid attention to. And when I left government, I served as one of the two civilian members on the advisory committee to the National Institute of Mental Health. In that job, I was the manic-depressive in a suit. You know, the guy from outside the medical community, from outside the National Institute of Mental Health, from outside all those drug companies, who could represent the general public.

I was lucky to have tremendous chances to help influence mental health policy and practices. When I was at the White House, I did grand rounds of medical schools. I'd go around and lecture to medical students, interns, and residents about how they should treat their patients. Because I had a fancy title, people listened more than they would have if I had just wandered in from off the street, like most of their patients.

After I left the government, I continued that kind of work, less so after my children were born. But I still do it and find it to be the most fulfilling work I've ever done. There's no question that nothing I've ever done has come close to giving me as much satisfaction as the time I spend doing advocacy, giving young people advice about how to handle the illness, and helping parents cope with it.

WHAT WORKS FOR BOB

- Finding a competent psychiatrist who prescribes the right medications and working with a talk therapist
- Having strong support from family and friends
- Moving from "I am this illness" to "I have this illness"
- Exercising
- Monitoring himself for early warning signs
- Confiding in people around him about his bipolar disorder so they know what to do if his mood becomes unstable
- Advocating for those with mental illness, which provides a sense of meaning for some of his earlier suffering

CHAPTER 7

CLIFF RICHEY

Former Top-Ranked Tennis Player

CLIFF RICHEY GREW UP IN A tennis family in Texas. His father was a tennis coach, and both Cliff and his sister Nancy played amateur and professional tennis in the 1960s and 1970s. In 1970, he was the top tennis player in the United States and winner of the international Grand Prix of Tennis, which was the world's first ranking tournament. He was also part of two US Davis Cup winning teams and was voted the most valuable player on the 1970 team. Other career highlights include winning forty-five tournament titles over a twenty-six-year career, including the Canadian Open (1969), South African Open (1972), US Indoors (1968), and US Clay Courts (1966 and 1970). He was also a US Open semifinalist (1970 and 1972) and a French Open semifinalist (1970).

Despite these impressive achievements, Cliff was plagued by self-doubt. He was known as the original "bad boy" of tennis, well before John McEnroe and Ilie Nastase. Only later did he realize that this behavior was exacerbated by episodes of depression. He documented his journey in the book *Acing Depression: A Tennis Champion's Toughest Match* (2010). In the foreword to Cliff's book, five-time US Open champion Jimmy Connors wrote, "What made Cliff Richey what he was on the tennis court has certainly carried over into this book. His story has taken a subject, depression—which has affected him personally—and put it out there for everyone to see. Few people even admit to having such a condition. But Cliff is not afraid to be bold and reveal what he has gone through and what it takes to get a handle on this disease" (2010, ii). Cliff now gives presentations about his experiences of managing his depression and finds this very fulfilling.

Cliff, could you tell me bit about your background and childhood?

I was born in San Angelo, Texas, and had a happy childhood. The only thing that was a bit unusual was the night terrors I experienced around ages nine and ten. I'd go to bed, and an hour later I'd appear to wake up. I'd still be asleep, but everybody thought I was awake. I had some extreme anxiety.

My whole family was involved in tennis in a very serious way. My father was a coach, and my sister, who is four years older than me, was a good player. I was only twelve when I decided I wanted to be a top player. It looked fun. I wasn't pushed. It was something I decided to do.

A lot of people think that if, for example, you have a father who's a doctor, he'll push you to become a doctor. But I made the decision to play tennis, and I'm glad I did. I dropped out of high school to focus on tennis. I always had a great affinity for all the older guys, like Roy Emerson. We had a common bond. We were hooked on tennis.

When I was fourteen we moved to Dallas, where I played in a lot of junior tournaments, and by sixteen I started playing in some fairly big men's events.

How was that?

From the time I was thirteen until my midtwenties, probably the biggest emotion I had was extreme anxiety. I was thrown in beyond my age division, and I was good enough to do it, but it created inordinate anxieties. Those anxieties drove me, because I thought that if I did well, they would lessen. But of course they came roaring back. And so anxiety was always driving me to do well.

It was a double-edged sword. The anxieties were uncomfortable, but I think they were a driving force. I think they were beyond the norm of everyday anxieties and were probably the precursor to depression. I constantly felt like I needed to do more and as though I might not be good enough. After winning a good match or tournament, I'd have somewhat of a high for a few days, but then I'd come back down. The worries would start over again because I'd wonder if I could match what I'd just done.

My dad was very much a perfectionist too. He thought that if you got good enough you could almost ward off defeat. I knew I was practicing hard. I was known as a hard worker as a kid and as an adult, and yet there was always that anxiety that I still wasn't good enough.

Did you have the opportunity to talk with anyone about that, or did you just think it was part of the deal?

I confided in my dad and my mom, but more my dad. He was my coach. I'd tell him I was feeling uneasy, and he was always approachable. So I had a great guy I could confide in, but he didn't truly understand, nor could anyone, really. You don't know what somebody else is feeling. It doesn't matter how close they are to you. But I did feel like I had somebody to talk to. Then later, when I was about twenty-one, I had extreme anxieties on the tour and possibly started having a bit of depression here and there.

I now know that my depression started in 1971 and was full-blown in 1973 through 1978. I had six years of hell in there.

My wife's mother, Bonnie, had psychiatric problems and actually ended up committing suicide. In 1969, I was feeling rocky enough to say to my wife, "I wonder if Bonnie could recommend a psychiatrist for me." I was feeling bad enough in different ways that I thought maybe I needed therapy, but I didn't end up seeing someone then.

Professional sport must be a very difficult environment because it depends so much on the results of matches. Can you tell me a bit about that?

In some ways, you learn to adapt. I've played in five hundred tournaments all over the world and fifteen hundred tennis matches, all either win or lose. If I had been a lawyer or a dentist or a doctor, I still probably would have had depression. It can't be blamed on my profession, though I was always going to be either a winner or a loser, and the losses stung pretty badly.

I can remember winning a big tournament called the US Indoors in Maryland in 1968. Nobody thought I could win because it was on a very fast surface and I was basically labeled as a clay courter. But I won it and was on an extreme high for two to three days. Then I came crashing down, and within a few days almost felt like I had gone into some depression.

Because I had gotten so high, the only place I could go was down, and I went a little too low. That might have been a warning sign, but it's a spiderweb, because you're used to playing through jet lag, through a bad cold, or even if you have a fever. So if you start feeling bad psychologically, you think it's just the game that you've chosen to play as a profession and that you have to overcome that too. Eventually it starts bleeding over into anxieties that may not be normal or depression that definitely isn't normal.

In the end, it helped me through my recovery to have that "never say die" attitude. I'd be damned if I wasn't going to get through the other side and be able to live a healthier life again. But it might also have been a drawback because I didn't admit to myself that I needed help.

Earlier you mentioned a conversation with your wife, where you wondered if her mother could recommend a psychiatrist. What led you to say that?

When I look back, I remember having extreme anxiety at the time. The funny thing is, if you look at my overall playing record for the fifteen years that I was on the regular tour, 1969 was probably the second-best year I had, results-wise.

Isn't that ironic?

Yeah. I knew that I was anxiety-ridden and probably even had a bit of depression at times. I just didn't feel good or right. I might have had a few bad tournaments that I thought I should have done better in. I was playing a lot of tennis that year. I probably played thirty weeks, all over Europe a couple of times, probably all over South America, and in South Africa. That contributed to some stress.

Do you think you considered getting a referral from your wife's mother because your sleep was affected?

I don't remember whether it was affecting my sleep that early. That definitely was a big problem starting in about 1973. I'd lie there forever, and took Valium to help me sleep, which was pouring fire on the coals. I drank beer every night, but limited it to four. I didn't want to have to play with a hangover, but I knew I could drink four and get happy. And then I was taking Valium to try to sleep and relax.

One night I took ten milligrams of Valium. The next day I was going to play against Alan Stone. I had always beaten him, and I felt like he didn't think he could beat me. The Valium didn't work, so I took another ten milligrams.

Before the night was over, I ended up taking at least forty milligrams of Valium. The last dose was probably at three in the morning, and I had about a ten o'clock midmorning match. When I walked onto the court, I could hardly feel my feet hit the carpet. We played indoors on a carpet, and I was probably legally DUI. Alan stayed true to form, and I somehow played decent enough to beat him pretty easily.

When did you decide that you needed help?

In the last few years, I've had people say things to me like, "Well, you were a well-known athlete at one time, and now you're depressed because you're a worn-out somebody." Wrong. The thing I prized and protected was my skill. I got depressed when I started losing some skill. My game started leaving me, and I knew it. I worked to get it back, but I never really did.

When my skills left me like that, I was still winning the odd tournament and still in the top thirty or forty players in the world, but I went from the top ten to the top whatever, and losing my skill was the spark point. At the time, I didn't know that I was in as bad a depression as I was. I was out of sync with everything and everybody. I took up golf when I was thirty years old, and I did pretty well in the senior tennis tour and played a lot of golf on the side. All of that helped, and I only had one flare-up that was really bad. In the fall of 1989 I was housebound for three months with depression, and I didn't seek help.

Were you living by yourself when you were housebound?

No, I was married to Mickey. I would hole up in my bedroom. I drank a bit more. I was a mess, but I just waited it out. Some stresses were hitting me. We figured that my tennis career was just about over, and I wasn't in as good financial shape as I thought. We put the house on the market. I had a thumb injury at that time and didn't know if I could play tennis or even golf, which was my passion.

I was starting to suffer all these losses all at once, and boom, I went into three or four months of depression.

How did Mickey respond to that?

She didn't add to the problem by trying to pick arguments or haranguing, and she tried to be as understanding as she could. She just kind of tiptoed around me. I'd always been an up-and-down person, but it got ridiculous.

How did you get over it?

My thumb started getting better, and I slowly got back to some of my activities. I could see that I was going to be able to play both tennis and golf. Other things started changing in my life, and I started feeling better. But I didn't relate that bad spell of 1989 to those last six years I played on the regular tour. I didn't realize that those times were connected, that both were depression, and that I'm predisposed. I just sort of let everything happen, as people sometimes do.

When did you get to the point that you felt you needed to ask for help?

The year of 1996. Until then I rocked along pretty well. I quit the senior tour in tennis in about 1991, and my golf was good enough for me to be invited to play in a celebrity golf tour.

In 1994, I started having some stomach problems and was a bit depressed. I was still drinking, and I also chewed tobacco. My mother asked me to quit both of those habits, and I took her seriously. I quit cold turkey on July 26, 1994.

January of 1996 is when I knew I needed help. I knew I needed to go to a counselor. I'm a Christian, but I didn't want to go to a pastor who counseled. I wanted someone who had a PhD in counseling people who need help, but who was a Christian too. I probably had thirty-five counseling sessions in 1996, and I learned a lot. I learned about codependency and the role my father played in my life. But the counselor only mentioned medication once. In December I could tell that the counselor was getting worn, and he wasn't helping me much anymore.

I went to my dermatologist, Harvey, who was a good family friend, and poured my heart out to him. I told him I wasn't enjoying life at all. A couple of days later, my wife happened to go in, and he told her that he had talked with me. He said, "Mickey, Cliff's in depression and he's trying to lick it on his own. I don't think he's going to be able to do it. He needs to be on medication." I didn't know that he had spent a year in the psych ward as part of his residency.

My wife came home and told me that, and I called Harvey at home. I asked him to call the prescription in and said, "I can't go any further down than I am right now. I'll try anything." He said, "You're halfway there if you're willing to take ownership of it and admit that you're having a problem."

So I went on medication, and then I started studying everything I could get my hands on to educate me about clinical depression. I read Peter Kramer's books, stuff on the Internet, and all kinds of stuff. I wanted to know what my brand of depression was and what my triggers were. What I did was almost like self-counseling. I started understanding what skill meant to me. I started understanding that I was too much of a perfectionist. I knew I was in trouble with depression because I didn't know how I was going to come out of it.

In December of 1996, I had black trash bags taped over my bedroom windows because I couldn't sleep. Come along late afternoon or early evening, I'd get really frightened. When you're in bad depression, you feel frightened all the time anyway. But I was convinced I might die just because I couldn't sleep, so I didn't want to know what time of day it was, just in case I could get some sleep. I had it nighttime all the time so I didn't have the pressure of *it's eight o'clock, nine o'clock, ten o'clock at night.*

Did the medication help?

My dermatologist put me on Elavil, which is an old-line tricyclic antidepressant. It wired me even more, so it felt like a freaking electrical socket was stuck up my ass. I couldn't handle it. My dermatologist recommended I see a psychologist, so I did, but I also went to my internist. I asked him to put me on Zoloft, which I had researched, and he prescribed it immediately.

I talked with the psychologist over the phone, and every few days he would ask me, "How do you feel on this dose?" I couldn't take fifty milligrams of the Zoloft at first because the nausea and other side effects were terrible. So I took fifteen to twenty milligrams for the first week and increased the dose in very small increments. It took four months to get any relief. Finally I settled in on a dosage of about two hundred milligrams, and I've been on that for thirteen and a half years. It was a miracle for me. I don't know what I would have done without the Zoloft.

Looking back, what do you think were the main factors contributing to your depression, beyond a biological predisposition?

I really believe that I am biologically predisposed. We now know that my grandfather fought it and self-medicated with alcohol. My mother suffered a bit that way too. So, genetically, I probably had a good pedigree.

Another factor was that my family was so rabid about tennis. We had total dedication. As a result, I think I was hyperaroused and hypervigilant, day to day, and maybe even minute to minute. I think those levels of cortisol and adrenaline, coupled with my skills leaving me, probably would have knocked anybody on their ass, even somebody who wasn't predisposed. But it was just an overall lifestyle, including hundreds and hundreds of jet lags.

Arthur Ashe, who was a good buddy of mine, once said, "I fear that Cliff Richey will burn out with the approach he takes to the game." And he was pretty on the money. I was so intense and hyper, so just crazed, really. But by and large, given the whole way it evolved, it would have been a miracle if I hadn't come down with depression.

What has been most helpful to you in battling depression?

I think I'll be on Zoloft the rest of my life. Of course age takes over too, but I can get up in the morning and have an hour and a half of drinking coffee slowly, watching a little news, and reading something. I also do a lot of journaling as part of therapy.

One of the biggest healers for me is thankfulness. I went through divorce after forty-one years of marriage and never saw it coming, yet I've weathered that. Through it all, I've used thankfulness as a weapon against depression. There have been mornings in the last few years where I've felt a little rocky—as if the black dog's after my ass. When that happens, I get a pen and paper out and start writing down every single thing I have to be thankful for, and that's *everything*—the air we breathe, food to eat, air-conditioning, you name it. I never have enough time in that day to finish that list.

Gratitude's huge. On the flip side, there aren't any magic wands. I tell people all the time that if you're deep in depression it can take a lot of hard work to get back to being healthy and feeling like you're living a good life. When I was at my sickest, I didn't want false hope. I just wanted some kind of hope. Medication is only one-third of it, maybe half, along with lifestyle. I try to be honest with people and say, "Recovery's not easy, but it's damn sure worth it."

After forty-one years of marriage, Mickey and you had obviously been through a lot. What led to the breakup?

I don't know. To be honest, I was blindsided. I didn't want the divorce. I will go to my grave not understanding it. When I was at my worst, from 1994 to 1997, she was terrific. I'd wake her up sometimes at three in the morning crying, and she'd come into my bedroom and hold my hand. She slept in another bedroom just to get some sleep.

I really thought that because we'd fought through a lot of things together over forty-one years, our marriage had gotten stronger and stronger. Then a few things went a little sideways that I would never have dreamed. If somebody had asked me three or four years ago if there was a chance my wife would file for divorce, I would have said no, no chance at all.

The last two years have been difficult. I had flare-ups of grief and depression at different times. It was like I lost my wife to death. It had a slightly different flavor than my other depressions, and when I could see that, my self-energy didn't get busted up so badly with the grief of the divorce as it did when I had full-blown depression. I was able to manage it all, but I will eventually ask God to his face, "Why?" because I still don't know.

Mickey never sat down with me and used the word "divorce." She almost picked an argument one day: October 3, 2008. It was over my book and how I wanted to try to get it published in the tennis community because those are my roots. She acted as if I was trying to pick an argument, then she got up and stormed out of the house, and I basically haven't seen her since. About seventeen days later, I got the papers handed to me at the door, and despite our forty-one years together, she never had a discussion with me as to why she did it.

That would be devastating for anyone, let alone someone with a predisposition to depression. I went through divorce as well, and it's bloody difficult. Why do you think you didn't plummet when that happened after such a long marriage?

Well, I did plummet, but I didn't plummet to the absolute depth. I was in absolute shock for the first six months. Through all my depressive episodes, I always felt that no matter how far down you get in the match, you could always keep fighting and pull it out. There is always a way out of any situation, even when you feel horrible.

The last two years have been difficult at times. After forty-one years, I can't really comprehend some of it. But it's like you're almost forced to move on or completely collapse. I've had some dark moments when I had real fears that the worst of my depression would come back and last a long time, and maybe I wouldn't recover this time. But I'm okay. I've been out the other side pretty long.

If you could go back to visit your eighteen-year-old self, what advice or recommendations would you give him?

That's a difficult question, because the biggest thing I wanted to do in life, from an early age, was to be an extremely successful tennis player, and I accomplished that. I would only go back and change my decision in 1969, when I thought about seeing a psychiatrist but didn't. However, I would only do the counseling, medication, and whatever other help they had in those days if I still could have had the successful career I had. I would go back and not drink. I would maybe try to find a different sleep medication than Valium.

If I had the knowledge I have today, I'd go back and try to look at life differently. If I had seen a sports psychologist, I think I could have been better in the time period when I was at my worst.

I needed help before I got it. I think it has to dawn on you that you do, in fact, have something wrong. I still don't know whether, even at the age of forty-two, it really sunk in that I had a problem and needed help. I would have been afraid to get help, but I now know why I needed it then.

I want to encourage people that there is help, that there is reason to hope, and that recovery is possible. In this day and age, thank goodness they have come up with better treatments and a greater variety of treatments. Recovery is doable. The battle with depression is winnable.

My father didn't really understand the disease, but he would call me most mornings. When the phone rang, I knew it was my dad. That meant everything to me. That's why, when people ask, "How do I deal with somebody who has it?" I say, "Love them. Let them know that you may not understand depression, but that you're there to try to understand it, and that together, you're going to do everything possible to get through it—and, darn it, you will."

Try to de-stress. Try to get good sleep. Don't drink. Don't take depressants, like Valium. Eat a good diet. Do something for somebody else. Have a sense of humor. Follow the Bible's advice. But remember that there's no magic bullet. I'm in a good recovery, but I call it "recovery," not "recovered."

You said you do about twelve presentations a year. What do you get out of that?

I decided that I wanted to be active and try to do a bit of something that's lacking. I've had people come up to me with tears in their eyes saying, "I have depression," or "My daughter has depression, and I appreciate you getting up and being willing to talk about it." It doesn't get much more powerful than that.

In my talks, I call depression a liar and a bully. It's a liar because God doesn't want us to be the way we are when we're so sick, with depression whispering nonstop in your ear, "Give up. It's not worth it. Nothing is worth living for anymore." That's a lie.

And depression is a bully because it comes at you when you're weak. But if you stand up to it like we're taught to stand up to schoolyard bullies, you're likely to find that it isn't as rough and tough as you think it is. It will stand down if we stand up to it.

WHAT WORKS FOR CLIFF

- Finally seeing a doctor and finding a medication that works for him
- Receiving emotional support from close family members
- Finding something to be grateful for, no matter what happens
- Eating well and giving up alcohol

CHAPTER 8

JENNIFER HENTZ MOYER

A Path Out of Postpartum Psychosis and Depression

JENNIFER HENTZ MOYER, THE YOUNGEST OF eight children in a family in a small Pennsylvania town, was raised by her mother after her father left the family when Jennifer was four years old. She attended a Catholic high school, where she met her future husband at the age of fifteen. She attended Florida Atlantic University and graduated with a degree in marketing in 1989, after marrying in 1988 at the age of twenty-one. She pursued a career in marketing, first at a banking title insurance company and then at a hospital, where she worked her way up to director of an occupational health program.

Jennifer had her only child in 1995, at which time she left the workforce. When her son was eight weeks old, she was diagnosed with postpartum depression and psychosis, a life-threatening mental illness. Eventually her illness developed into depression, and she struggled to find the right balance of medication, support, and coping skills.

In 2000, Jennifer joined Postpartum Support International (PSI) in order to help others suffering from postpartum psychosis and postpartum depression, and she ultimately became the northwest Florida coordinator for the organization. In 2003, she was finally correctly diagnosed as having bipolar disorder, postpartum onset. After a complete neuropsychological evaluation in 2006, she started on the right balance of medications, which has contributed to her current happy and stable life. Jennifer is now a mental health advocate, working to increase awareness and education about mental health issues and promote their prevention and treatment.

Jennifer, could you tell me a bit about your early childhood?

I was born in Pennsylvania, in a small town outside of Philadelphia. I'm the youngest of eight children. Thankfully, my mom wanted a lot of children. I was shy, and my two brothers and five sisters protected me. My father left the family when I was just four, so that was a traumatic time for everyone in my family. Because I was so young, I don't remember much of it. The two oldest were married and out of the house, but the rest of us were still living at home when he left. I was too young to understand. Obviously, the lack of a father in the house was difficult, especially on my mother. When I was about nine years old, I did get to meet my father for what seemed like the first time. Even though he was a stranger, it was nice to know I had a daddy. I only saw him maybe once a year at that point because he lived in Florida.

What was it like growing up without a father?

I guess I didn't know any different. I went to a Catholic school, and that was difficult because at the time divorce wasn't common, at least in our area. That was challenging, and I remember sometimes thinking it would be easier if my father was dead, as opposed to having left my family. It would have made it easier to manage the stigma. As I got older, the family became more open about talking about it: the fact that he had left and what the situation was like. My mom used to reminisce about how things were before he left, and she always said he was a good man and a good father. Looking back on it, she believed he'd had a mental breakdown. He met somebody else and went on to marry her. He was married to her until he died in December 2008.

What reason were you given about why your father left?

We knew he went off and married somebody else after he and my mom were divorced. Maintaining such a large family was overwhelming for him. There was a lot of stress in his job at the time. My mom was so busy with the family that she probably didn't see a lot of the signs. I think it was easier for him to walk away than to stay and deal with it at that point.

How was school for you?

School was a good environment. As mentioned, I was shy, but I had a few close friends. I also met my husband, Mike, at fifteen, and that changed my life in a big way. My mom liked him so much that she bent her rule of no dating before age sixteen. She let me go out on my first date when I was just two months shy of sixteen.

How did the relationship with Mike change you?

It was uplifting and gave me security. In retrospect, I'm sure a lot of it was because I didn't have a male figure when I was growing up, and there were times I was confused. I broke up with Mike a couple of times in high school, but we always managed to drift back together. He went to a public school in the area that was one of the rivals of my Catholic school. He was two years ahead of me in school.

What did you study at college?

I majored in accounting for the first two years, but found it boring, so I switched to marketing. I graduated in December 1989. There weren't many college graduates in my family, and I was very proud of accomplishing that. Mike and I got married in 1988, when I was still in college. At that time, only two of my sisters had graduated from college. Other siblings had taken courses, but I was the third out of the eight to graduate from college.

What work did you do after you graduated?

I took a job with a banking title insurance company, and I enjoyed that. Later I got a job in marketing at a hospital. I loved that job. I worked my way up over several years, and not long before my son was born, in 1995, I was promoted to program director, which was great. I worked right up until I had my son.

Before you had your son, you had a miscarriage. Is that right?

Yes. I had the miscarriage in 1993, and it was the most difficult thing I'd gone through at that point. I was just eight weeks pregnant, and my husband and I had told everybody that we were expecting. It would have been the first grandchild on my husband's side. I knew it could happen, but I didn't think it would happen to me because my mother had had so many pregnancies. It had taken a year for me to get pregnant, so we were very excited. Then the miscarriage happened, and we had to tell everybody. It was overwhelming.

I think it was harder for me to get past than it was for my husband. It was hard on him too, but he was able to put it behind him sooner, whereas I had a lot of guilt. I think a lot of women feel like that when they have a miscarriage. I was never directed to any support or any grief counseling, and looking back, I think that would have been very appropriate, but we managed to get through it.

Of course, the thing I wanted most after that was to get pregnant again. Almost exactly a year to the day after I had my miscarriage, I first heard my son's heartbeat with the second pregnancy. The miscarriage made me very reserved during my second pregnancy. I wasn't as excited because I knew something could go wrong, and we waited twelve weeks before we told anybody. It had a much different feel because of the miscarriage.

How did you adjust to life with a child?

The first ten days after my son was born, I was exhausted, but I started doing better as the weeks passed. Sometimes I cried for no reason, which I was expecting. They call it "the baby blues," and about 80 percent of mothers experience it. My sister's encouragement helped me get through that, and after about two weeks, I was doing great. I had bonded with my son, and breastfeeding was going well. My mother had arrived about ten days after my son was born, and she stayed with me and helped around the house while I was taking care of the baby. I had a lot of support for the first six weeks. I was happy—maybe a little too happy, but I didn't know that at the time.

When my mom had to leave, I had mixed feelings. I wanted her to go so I could do things on my own, but because my husband was back at work, I knew I'd be alone. After she left, the reality started to sink in. I started feeling so isolated and fearful. I'd have this sudden feeling that something was going to happen to me and someone was going to take my baby. It came on suddenly, and I didn't tell anybody because I was afraid. I didn't get any sleep. I went two nights without sleep, and by the third night I didn't trust anyone, not even my husband, so I wouldn't let him hold the baby. He contacted my doctor and I spoke to her. She offered to come to the house, and at that point I thought she was the only one I could trust, so I said yes. My husband had to take the phone from me to give her directions because I couldn't concentrate well enough to do that. I guess she called an ambulance, because people started coming. I was getting more and more paranoid and just kept holding the baby.

Paramedics showed up and I didn't know who they were, so my fear that someone was going to take my baby was actually materializing before me. My doctor was able to get the baby from me as the police pulled me to the ground. No one explained anything to me, so when I was taken to the hospital, I continued to think they were trying to kill me and that everything that I feared was coming to be.

I had an overwhelming fear that I needed to protect my son because something or someone was trying to take him from me. It was obviously a false belief, but it came on like a powerful wave from out of nowhere. At the hospital, I was eventually told I had postpartum depression. I didn't think I was depressed. I felt paranoid and distrustful. They gave me some medicine, and I flushed it down the toilet because I still thought they were trying to kill me. I wanted to get out of the hospital and get back to breastfeeding my son. Then everything would be fine.

Once I was stable, they discharged me without any medicine. But two weeks later my sleep became disrupted again. One day at church, I started to hear the priest saying strange things. It sounded like he was talking about evil and sacrificing, and there appeared to be two lines going to the altar. That was the first time I had a hallucination, so I wound up in the hospital a second time and was finally correctly diagnosed as having postpartum psychosis, which is similar to postpartum depression in some respects, but very rare and life-threatening, and much more serious. Getting a name for my problem helped me feel like I wasn't crazy—that everything I was experiencing was part of an illness I had. They put me on medication, and that helped stabilize me.

Was it antipsychotic medication?

Yes. The doctor also gave me antidepressants, and ultimately I wound up getting depressed. I was stabilized from the psychosis.

The doctor was a good clinician and adjusted my medicine a lot because I'd go up and down. I'd do better, and then I'd do worse. Finally, when my son was about fourteen months old, I went back to work full-time because our medical bills were getting out of hand. Our insurance wasn't covering my medical expenses because I had a mental illness. At that time they didn't recognize it as a medical condition, so there was a lot of financial stress on top of everything else.

At the end of April my son got sick. Whenever he got sick I felt so overwhelmed and guilty, especially when I was working. I thought if I weren't working, he wouldn't have gotten sick. Anyway, he was at day care and I was at home. I was in a terrible panic. I had this awful sense of evil. I was scared to death and couldn't sit still. I was on the edge, and if I could have used a gun, I would have probably used it on myself. It was as if my actions were detached. *I gotta sleep, I gotta rest* kept racing through my head, so I took my medicine and drank an old wine cooler that was in the fridge. I'd never done drugs and I only had an occasional drink, so this was unusual for me. The last thing I remember was talking to my husband on the phone and telling him what I'd done.

He raced home, and then some paramedics showed up. They took me to the hospital. I don't remember any of that. I don't remember them pumping my stomach, and I don't remember them having to restart my heart. After I was stable, they did electroconvulsive therapy. After the treatment I got sick and started vomiting. I didn't know it was called electroconvulsive therapy at that time; I just knew they were vibrating my head and I was getting sick afterward. I just kind of went with the flow at that point.

After I got out of the hospital I stayed with my dad for a while, but I had another panic attack because I was away from my son and husband. I ended up in a different hospital because my dad lived about an hour north of the hospital I was in before. This hospital, which was closer to my dad's, was a lot more positive. I met a female doctor who was a mother. She wasn't an expert on postpartum psychosis, but she seemed to understand. I felt like I had been judged by some of the medical community, but she didn't look at me like that. They tried all kinds of medications, and nothing seemed to work long term. But by the time my son was about eighteen months old, I felt like I was starting to see a light at the end of the tunnel. I wasn't back to the way I remembered myself being before I had my son, but I started feeling hopeful.

Unfortunately, it took about nine hospital stays over the course of two and a half years before I was doing well. I stopped having relapses and was off medication by the time my son was two and a half, but it was a long process.

What was it that gave you hope?

The female doctor at the hospital and a counselor I was seeing. We also were referred to a licensed marriage and family therapist. My husband and I saw him together, and he helped us start focusing on us as a family. I had started working part-time again at a company that I loved working for, and I lowered my stress. Also, my son was in preschool, which gave me a break, but it was hard not being with him all the time, especially when I was trying to recover. I can't say I felt better immediately, but pieces of the puzzle started coming together.

I knew I was getting better because I started laughing again. Prior to that I couldn't laugh. The antipsychotic medication was very numbing. Sometimes it made me feel like I wanted to crawl out of my skin, and other times I felt I was just going through the motions like a zombie. I think getting off that medication helped too.

At what point did anyone discuss a diagnosis of bipolar disorder with you?

In 1999, right before we moved and when my son was almost four. I had been off medication for a while, and I had been doing really well. We went camping, and I guess the excitement of the trip was overwhelming. I felt I was sensing evil and had so many fears that I hardly slept. I felt like I was supposed to help somebody, and as we were driving past a rundown airfield, I told my husband to stop. I suddenly felt like I had to get out and pray. He wouldn't stop, but he was going pretty slow, so I jumped out of the van and started walking toward the runway. I was praying and praying and walking and walking, and I walked all the way across it.

I saw my husband in the distance talking to somebody, and when I got across the runway, there was a police car. It followed me for a while, then one of the officers got out and came up to me. He was very kind and said, "Let's take you to a safe place." So I wound up in the hospital again. Apparently this is when a doctor first brought up the idea that I might have a problem other than postpartum psychosis.

I went back to Florida and was put on a mood stabilizer, but no one ever directly said, "You have bipolar disorder." They may have discussed it with my husband, but they never discussed it with me. Before our move, I saw a doctor who suggested that when I got to the new location, I should find a doctor to talk to about medication options. But again, no one said, "We're giving you this medicine because we think you have bipolar disorder," which still frustrates me. The medical community doesn't recognize that even if people have an illness, they can be educated and understand what is going on.

After we moved, I found another doctor and was put on Neurontin, a mood stabilizer. I did pretty well, and later that year I contacted Postpartum Support International. I started educating myself and learning about postpartum psychosis and postpartum depression. I wanted to help other people. I contacted PSI and happened to speak with Jane Honikman, the founder of the organization. At that point she was answering the phones, and I told her I'd do what I could to help.

I started getting more involved with PSI and ultimately became the northwest Florida coordinator. In 2001, there was a case in Texas where a woman, Andrea Yates, who had postpartum psychosis, drowned her children. It threw me so far for a loop. Having gone through the illness myself, my heart broke. It had been five years since I went through it, and I'd thought we'd made progress. When that happened, I was devastated. PSI supported Yates, and that was when postpartum mood disorders began to be discussed more widely here in the United States.

When my husband was out of the country in November 2003, I had to be hospitalized. He was going to be away for six weeks, which was the longest he had ever been gone. Toward the end of his trip, I sought support because I was struggling to keep up with the house and the meals. Unfortunately, it backfired on me. When I came home from taking my son to the pediatrician, my pastor and two police cars were at my house. They said they were going to take my son, and that I would probably be "Baker Acted." The Baker Act is a Florida law that allows authorities to forcibly hospitalize people. I wasn't homicidal and I wasn't suicidal, which you supposedly had to be, but the police came in and forcibly handcuffed me.

I was being treated like a criminal and felt frantic. I still have a scar on my wrist from the handcuffs. Thankfully, they had already taken my son to a neighbor who volunteered to help, so he wasn't put in foster care. But I still had the same fear that I had after he was born. I didn't know what they were going to do to me, and I thought they were trying to harm me.

I was so scared, but I had a lot more knowledge, so I was telling them, "I know my rights. You can take me to be voluntarily evaluated," but they refused to listen to me. This was a small county, and the police officers weren't highly trained or educated in the area of mental health. I ended up in a facility with a lot of addicts and people without insurance.

How long were you there?

About ten days. In the meantime, my husband came home, and the Department of Children and Families told him that if he didn't sign a restraining order against me, he would lose his son. They didn't understand mental illness, and they manipulated the situation. My husband understood me and the illness better than anyone, and if he had been home, none of this would have happened. But he did what they told him.

In January 2004, I finally saw a doctor who started educating me about bipolar disorder and postpartum psychosis. He showed me a review on bipolar disorder and postpartum psychosis published in the *American Journal of Psychiatry*. From that article, I learned that a woman with postpartum psychosis, whether she has a history of bipolar disorder or not, should be treated as if she has bipolar disorder. If she's on antidepressants alone, she will have more cyclic moods, which I did. Women in this situation should be given a mood stabilizer right away. That didn't happen for me until two years after my son's birth. Several months earlier, I also saw an expert in New York who diagnosed me with bipolar disorder, postpartum onset.

In November 2006, I had a relapse when I went to a family event. It was stressful, and my sleep was disrupted. I had to go back in the hospital, but everything was finally done right. They did a complete neuropsychological evaluation, medical testing, and a sleep disorder study to ensure an accurate diagnosis. Those tests weren't new, so I don't know why some of them weren't done earlier. They prescribed Lamictal, a mood stabilizer, and I also took Klonopin for a little while, as I needed it to help me sleep. That was over three years ago and I haven't had any problems since.

What do you do to keep yourself stabilized apart from taking medication?

I exercise regularly. I have a mini trampoline, which I love, and I try to do that every day. I do some strength training once or twice a week. Since then, God has brought people into my path who I can help. I'm no longer a coordinator for PSI, but I have helped people who are in depression. I take fish oil and some supplements that I believe to be helpful, and I try to eat right. Nutrition has been important, as is getting the right kind of therapy from a caring professional. For me, having a female provider has always been better because women understand what it's like to be female. The therapy has been so helpful. When my life gets stressful, sometimes it's better to talk to someone who is more objective and won't take things personally.

My spiritual support is important. I've always believed in God, but after I recovered from postpartum psychosis I started getting closer and closer to God. I now know that fear doesn't come from God, so my fear is gone. Obviously, I get nervous about certain things, but I don't have fear, and I used to have a lot of it.

Being a spiritual person, do you have any thoughts about why God might have put you through that?

I don't think he necessarily put me through it. I think it may have happened to me because the ability to help other people flows out of suffering. I'm a stronger person because of everything I've been through, and I think I'm a more complete person. I'm more understanding, and I've been able to help other people, which in turn has helped heal me.

When I was doing the coordinator work for PSI, it was so rewarding to hear women say, "You're the only person I can talk to who understands what I'm going through." I know how alone you can feel. Even though I had an excellent doctor, support, and therapy, I never got to talk to anyone who had gone through postpartum psychosis until I got involved with PSI. That makes a huge difference. When someone has walked a similar path, they can understand. But if they've never felt the darkness and despair or mania, they can't understand.

If you could go back to when you were pregnant with your son, what advice would you give yourself?

Knowing what I know now, I'd tell myself to have realistic expectations. You can't do it all, despite what our society tries to convey. You can't successfully be a full-time career person and a full-time mother and wife. I would warn myself about sleep deprivation especially, because I didn't think that would be such a problem. I'd also recommend getting support from someone who understands the illness. And if I could go back, I would have sought an accurate diagnosis earlier.

How would you describe your life now?

It's very balanced, and I've worked hard to achieve that. Through my journey, I've learned what does and doesn't work for me. Now I'm at peace and I feel happy. Journaling and writing have been a healing part of my journey too. Sometimes just getting your thoughts on paper can help release things so you can set them aside. I understand my illness better now, and I know I have to protect my sleep. I learned the hard way how to maintain wellness. That doesn't mean something won't happen, because you never know, but I feel like things have come together for me.

WHAT WORKS FOR JENNIFER

- Finally getting an accurate diagnosis
- Taking the right medications
- Having the support and understanding of her husband
- Exercising and eating well
- Receiving emotional support from a female doctor
- Taking strength from her spiritual beliefs
- Helping others going through the same thing

CHAPTER 9

GREG MONTGOMERY

NFL Player with the Houston Oilers and Baltimore Ravens

GREG MONTGOMERY GREW UP ON THE Jersey Shore. He was very involved in sports from an early age until he badly injured his back. He was told he'd never play contact sports again. This was a huge disappointment for him, but he quickly set a goal of becoming a punter in the NFL, since that position usually doesn't involve contact. In 1983, he went to Penn State and later moved to Michigan State. In 1988, he was drafted by the Houston Oilers and played with that team for six seasons. While with the Oilers, he experienced performance anxiety for the first time. After signing a contract with the Detroit Lions in 1994 and playing there for a year, he lost interest in playing and took a year off from the game.

In 1996, he signed a contract with the Baltimore Ravens and began to experience heightened anxiety and depression. In 1997, he had his first episode of mania and self-medicated with alcohol.

His bipolar mania brought with it grandiose plans that led to a multitude of business ventures, not all of them successful. Greg went into rehab a couple of times before finally quitting alcohol, and now maintains a healthy diet and lifestyle. He also finds a great deal of satisfaction in helping others who are struggling with bipolar disorder.

Greg, could you tell me a bit about your childhood?

I grew up in Shrewsbury, New Jersey, a small town on the Jersey Shore. My family was upper-middle-class, and I had a pretty good childhood. I was very active in sports, and during my childhood, I based most of my happiness on my success in sports. My mom was a stay-at-home mom, and she did a great job. She was the backbone of the family. My dad was a hardworking self-made guy who worked on Wall Street. He played college football, so we had a lot in common. He provided everything a kid could desire, but the family atmosphere tended to be very competitive and sometimes sarcastic, and that fueled my competitiveness and insensitivity to others.

What sports did you enjoy playing?

When I was younger I played baseball, hockey, football, tennis, golf, and a bit of basketball. Hockey was my number one sport. I liked the competition, getting the heart rate going, and getting out there and banging heads with the guys. Being successful in hockey was a great way of building self-esteem, and I had success at a very early age.

Hockey was your favorite sport?

Yes. During my high school years I was playing hockey, football, and baseball, and in baseball, I had some honors as the designated hitter and pitcher. I also had success on the football field playing linebacker and tight end. But when I hurt my lower back during my junior season in 1982, I was told by a New York orthopedic surgeon that I'd never play contact sports again.

That must have been a huge blow.

It was. I was devastated. I had to quit hockey and reinvent myself at an early age. Because I couldn't play contact sports anymore, I decided to focus on kicking and punting. When I came home from New York City, I wrote on a piece of stationery that my goal in life was to become a professional specialist in the NFL, and I did it.

Who gave you support during that time? Were your parents supportive?

My parents were very supportive. They sent me to kicking camps. I was told by the doctor in New York that there were two options for my recovery: I could either be in a body cast for twelve months, or I could swim laps every day after school and rehabilitate that way. So I decided to swim the laps. My mom picked me up at my lunch period every day and took me to swim at the local YMCA.

Eventually you returned to sports, but in a different role. How was that for you?

Due to the position change, I was forced to deal with stigma at an early age. In college and the NFL, punters and kickers are always painted as outcasts. I was a linebacker trapped in a punter's body, and I took an aggressive approach to my work ethic. Being a perfectionist, I focused on the fundamentals of kicking and punting. I just embraced it. At first I felt a little alienated, but I just brushed it off and internalized it. Still, it was difficult making the transition, especially because I'd enjoyed being part of a team and was suddenly forced into the role of an individual. Sometimes it was tough, but my teammates were supportive. It got much easier when I started to have success.

During your high school years, were there any issues around your mood?

Not really. After the injury, I obviously dealt with a bit of mild depression. But once I embraced the goal of being a punter or kicker, first in college and then the NFL, things got easier.

What were some of the highlights of your time at Penn State?

I was proud of being the first punter in Penn State history to receive a full scholarship. I met a lot of quality guys during my time there. I was a kickoff specialist and backup punter. But I was immature and ran into trouble off the field. I was somewhat of a hell-raiser—too much fun and too much drinking. I decided I wanted to start over and ended up transferring to Michigan State.

Did you enjoy that more?

Yes. It was a lot better fit for me. That was where my dad went to school. I had to sit out a year and earn a scholarship. Playing for coach George Perles, my father's teammate at Michigan State, was a treat. I worked hard and ended up being a three-time All–Big Ten punter and two-time All-American punter. The ultimate highlight was when the team won the Rose Bowl in 1988.

Were there any lowlights during your time there?

Yes. I used to get into scuffles every now and then. I'd get a little too rambunctious after cocktails. Those are definitely things I'm not proud of. It was just kind of the lifestyle. You know, work hard, play hard. And when you mix alcohol with testosterone, you tend to get into trouble.

In retrospect, did you have any issues around bipolar in college?

I don't think so. I definitely wore my emotions on my sleeve. I was a high-energy guy, and I went out of my way to prove that I was part of the team. I was just really driven. I never felt any full-blown mania at any time, or any depression. I didn't have any mental health issues at that point.

When you finished college, how did you choose which team to go to?

I was drafted in the third round of the 1988 NFL draft by the Houston Oilers. Making the transition from college to pro was difficult for me. The speed of the athletes was a lot faster. I had a somewhat tough time in my first professional season.

Did you start to feel settled and happy in Houston?

Yes. I was All-Pro my second season. But I still always based my happiness on my performance on the football field. If I had a good game, I was happy. But if I didn't have a good game, I didn't take it so well. I was so competitive and wanted to be the best. I struggled with performance anxiety. Every single game, I had a tough time going out there and getting into the flow of the game.

How did you overcome that performance anxiety?

Just by breathing. Simply knowing that I was always well prepared helped a lot. But I still always had to deal with anxiety. I just went out and fought through it by really focusing on technique. Most of the time I was successful, but it was tough at times. I was always trying to be perfect and gain the respect of the coaches and other players.

How would you summarize your time at Houston, and why did you decide to move on?

I played six years with Houston and enjoyed a lot of success. I led the NFL in punting average three times during those years. Unfortunately, my contract negotiations broke down in 1994, and they ended up signing another punter. Not getting a new contract with the Oilers was very disappointing. I ended up signing a one-year contract with the Detroit Lions. After that season I quit. I just lost my urge to play. That year I took off, 1995, was when I started feeling serious anxiety and depression.

Did you seek any help?

I don't recall seeking any help. I just dealt with it. I internalized it. I was extremely stressed-out and self-medicated with alcohol and cannabis a lot of the time. I remember being in a fog. I opened a successful lounge in Houston called Strict-9. During that time, I met a girl and fell in love, and my depression and anxiety lifted. I felt like myself again, and I decided to return to football. After playing golf with a couple of buddies from the Oilers, I was looking through the paper and I noticed the money punters were making in 1995. I bet my buddies that I could play again. Not long afterward, I made my comeback with the Baltimore Ravens.

I had a pretty good year with the Ravens in 1996. But by the end of the season my body started breaking down again. I was getting a pain in my lower back, hips, and hamstrings, and I started using pain medication during the latter part of the year. After the season, I went to Miami and was active in the electronic music scene. All of a sudden, I had my first experience of mania.

Do you think anything contributed to the mania coming on?

The stress of the season took a big toll on me. I was so relieved when the season was over and I just let loose. I probably wasn't sleeping, working out, or eating as much as I should have. I was also taking pain pills, partying late, self-medicating with cannabis, and experimenting with MDMA. All of those could have been contributing factors. I just wanted the pain and stress to go away.

What happened during that manic episode?

I suddenly had all this energy. It felt like I had a spiritual awakening. I didn't want to play football anymore. Believe it or not, I wanted to save the world through electronic music. I wanted to start music festivals that would bring all cultures together and create a cumulative healing effect by stressing nonviolence and compassion. I definitely got a little extravagant with my goals and aspirations.

Did your friends notice that something was different?

Definitely. My friends, family, and teammates saw what was happening. With my first manic break, I thought this was the "new me." I was enlightened. I was on a roll. I was entertaining all these different investment opportunities and my mind was racing out of control. I even said I wanted to take an IQ test because I felt smarter. My mind was working on overload.

A lot of people noticed the change in the way I dressed and how I talked. I got some new tattoos. I would dye my hair and paint my fingernails. I started hanging out with a diverse European crowd and was dating a fashion stylist from Milan. I was kind of flipping my nose to society with my newfound energy and spirit. It was as if I was shedding my old self. I determined that my old self had died and I'd transcended into this new person. I decided that I wasn't going to be the person I used to be. It was almost like a delayed adolescence. Regardless, it had all the symptoms of a spiritual awakening.

Was there any delusional thinking?

I don't know if it was necessarily delusional as much as it was grandiose. The people I was hanging out with actually ended up starting the world-renowned Ultra Music Festival. I was euphoric and didn't want to identify myself with football anymore. I rebelled against it and was planning on giving my signing bonus back.

I also went on some spending sprees. I bought fifty thousand dollars of John Lennon's Bag One art. I didn't know it, but this was my first real experience with mania. It's like a six-year-old driving a Lamborghini. Eventually you're going to crash. And crash I did.

How did you crash?

I just woke up one morning and all my confidence and bravado had evaporated. I immediately thought to myself, *Oh my god, what have I done? Who is this person I'm trying to portray?* I panicked. From that point on, a huge black cloud followed me everywhere I went.

When I was manic, I enjoyed all the attention. People noticed I'd been acting differently. I was extremely energetic and felt like I had been reborn. I really didn't think I had a problem. I was just being extravagant and a little over-the-top. But when my depression kicked in, I panicked. All of a sudden, I didn't know what to do. That's when suicidal thoughts started to creep in.

When you crashed, did you seek help from anyone?

Yes. Prior to reporting to camp, I wasn't eating or sleeping properly, and I'd lost a lot of weight. My teammates and coaches were worried about me. It was terrible. I had a panic attack right before a preseason game. I couldn't catch the football. I couldn't concentrate and was seeing tunnel vision. But I had to go out and play a game. I was given Ativan to help me work through it. I actually ended up having a good game. But it was scary because I was shaking the whole time. I couldn't feel my hands. I genuinely thought I was going to die.

Did you see a doctor then?

Yes. They brought a psychiatrist in, and he prescribed some medication. One of the medications actually made me manic again, so they finally determined I had bipolar disorder. That was when I first started trying different psychiatric drugs to remedy the situation.

It must have been unbelievably difficult to continue high-level professional football while going through all those medication adjustments.

It was chaos—a year from hell. I just dealt with it the best I could. I had to fight through the stress every day. After getting through the 1997 season, I cleaned up my act. I quit drinking and quit smoking cannabis. I was in great shape and was excited for the 1998 season. After mini camp in May, I was asked to go out on the field to film a commercial for the Ravens. They were filming me punting the football from the ground up, and I accidentally kicked the camera. I broke my foot in two places and wasn't able to punt for two months. I was disappointed, but I stayed positive and went to camp in July determined to work through the injury. I did pretty well that preseason, even with a broken foot. Unfortunately, I got cut from the Ravens, and that was the end of my career.

But your whole life had been football. What happened when you were cut from the team?

Lack of good management led to the demise of my lounge in Houston. I had invested in a record label in 1997 and I was trying to break into the music industry. In addition to electronic music, I was producing a band, distributing their CDs, and putting on concerts. I dabbled in a bunch of different types of businesses. Making the transition from pro football player to John Q. Citizen was difficult for me. I was just trying to find myself, and in retrospect I see that I was lost.

Was your mood under control then?

It was somewhat under control. I did self-medicate with cannabis and alcohol. That probably didn't help, but it seemed to work at the time. When it comes to bipolar, alcohol and drugs work until they don't. When I was depressed, I'd just stay in the house. But eventually the cycle would break and I'd snap out of it. My on-again, off-again love affair with drugs and alcohol led me to go into rehab in 2000. In later years, doctors told me that my mood disorders could have been triggered by the stress and concussions I got while playing in the NFL.

What was the lead-up to going to rehab?

I was doing too many drugs and partying too much. I was drinking away the pain and just wasn't in a good space. It wasn't a real addiction situation as much as abuse. I think it had a lot to do with my depression. I'd think about how my career ended and always had aspirations of making another comeback. It seemed that football was my way of feeding my ego and making me feel whole. It's all I really knew how to do.

Was rehab helpful?

It was. I learned a lot about myself and the many things I needed to work on. I stayed sober for about a year and a half.

How did you do that?

I chose to abstain from alcohol and drugs. I was also really working the 12-step program at the time. I've always preferred group programs to one-on-one counseling because they give you a chance to help others. Not giving up was a matter of internal fortitude, or self-will. My family has always been very supportive. Most of my family is sober. My sister's been sober for twenty-five years and both of my parents are sober. I received a lot of support at the time. My dad actually got sober at the same time I did. I told him, "If I'm going to get sober, it's your turn too," and he agreed to it.

What happened next?

I moved down to Baton Rouge, Louisiana, where I consulted as a kicking coach at Louisiana State University. I developed the "set and pull" technique that I teach today. I had a lot of success with a punter named Donnie Jones, who currently plays with the Houston Texans.

Was working around the sidelines of football a good substitute for you? Did it bring the same sort of pleasure as playing, or not as much?

It was only a part-time gig, but I definitely enjoyed it. Seeing the kids excel was always a good feeling. Unfortunately, I still felt the urge to self-medicate. I tried to relive my past glory and spark up nostalgia, and part of that was drinking. It was something everybody did while I was playing football. It was part of the culture. I was obviously still trying to find myself. I ended up getting a DUI in 2004, but I didn't learn my lesson, because I only briefly stopped drinking after that incident.

In 2005, I went into the mortgage business with a friend from Michigan and did that for about four and a half years. That was the first real job I had after retiring from football. We answered phones and took mortgage applications. It was pretty simple work, but my buddy definitely went out of his way to give me the team of people I needed to help me get through the day and actually close loans. I was lucky. It was definitely a special arrangement.

Did you enjoy that work?

Yes. At the time it was good for me. I enjoyed the people I worked with. I had the option to leave work and go lie down if I got stressed-out. The owner was great and gave me a lot of support. It was nice getting a paycheck, but I still dealt with depression and anxiety. I wasn't taking my diagnosis as seriously as I should have because I still drank a few times a week.

The company went out of business in 2009. After that, I continued to build my coaching and consulting company and had success with quite a few clients. But during that time I started to get manic again and made some rash decisions, like tapping into my 401(k) with the NFL. In retrospect, it probably wasn't a great idea. I was on a bunch of medications and dealt with a lot of weight gain, constipation, and difficulty concentrating. That was when I started to research some of the medications I was taking.

Looking back, what are the things you know you can do to help keep you well?

I realized that I really need to take care of myself. I make sure I eat very healthy foods. I believe there are a lot of toxins in junk food and many genetically modified foods. I make sure I get good sleep, and I exercise daily. I do a lot of prayer and meditation as well.

I currently do a lot of reading. I'm focused on helping other people who are dealing with what I've been through. I've put my hand on the stove many times, and I've finally realized that it's hot. I can't self-medicate anymore. I've realized that I have to identify my moods and take the proper measures when they're cycling. Whether it be a depressive or hypomanic state, I need to stay positive and take care of myself.

I've looked closely into the spiritual side of life lately. I've made a conscious decision to revamp my life and my values. I was very materialistic in the past. I searched for external pleasure and engaged in activities that would appease my senses. Now I've learned that things like money, power, and sex are transient. I've decided that I need to look within in order to find peace of mind and happiness. It's always there for us if we stay present. But when we're constantly rehashing the past and thinking about the future, we can't enjoy today. So, being present, enjoying the day minute by minute, is a technique I use to avoid negative thoughts.

I've recently started thinking about my legacy and what I've contributed to others. A lot of people ask me if I would change anything, and I have to say no, because if I did, I wouldn't be in the space I am now. I had to experience all of those highs and lows in order to be the person I am today. I currently share my vision of hope and my experiences with others to help them avoid having the kinds of confrontations I've had with my friends and family.

What do you say to people who have had issues with their family?

I try to urge them to focus on open communication, active listening, and willingness to change their behavior. Change is difficult for anybody. I truly believe that the family system is part of bipolar, and that adjustments need to be made across the board. Getting into the ERIC [Everyone Remains In Control] program, which offers workshops to help people with mental health conditions and their families work better together, has been fulfilling. It's about developing tools to get you through each day, and developing tools to promote effective communication within the family.

You mentioned the importance of being present and mindful. How do you do it—how do you stay in the moment?

I've read *The Power of Now*, by Eckhart Tolle, many times. The way I stay present is by always trying to take note of my surroundings. I start by doing breathing exercises and trying to stay in the moment as I follow my breath. And when thoughts of the past or an imagined future come into my mind, I actually say "stop" out loud. That tends to help me shut down my overactive thinking. But really it's just a matter of focusing on the present moment and enjoying the people you're with and the activity you're doing. The moral to the story is that all we really have is this present moment.

If you could go back and give your eighteen-year-old self advice, what would that be?

To stay away from drugs and alcohol would probably be my most important advice. I would also advise myself to appreciate people for who they are—to avoid being judgmental, and try to extend unconditional love toward others. All we can really work on is our self and being the most productive person possible.

Other than *The Power of Now,* have any other books had a major influence on you?

Yes. *The Handbook to Higher Consciousness,* by Ken Keyes Jr., promotes moving past our lower states of consciousness. These are the centers of sensation, power, and security—all of the ego-based desires that we have. Most of the books that I've been reading are about mindfulness and staying present. That's really the ultimate goal. I also believe that like attracts like, and recently enjoyed *The Law of Attraction,* by Esther and Jerry Hicks. *The Road Less Traveled,* by M. Scott Peck, is about the psychology of love, traditional values, and spiritual growth. I also enjoy Wayne Dyer's *Change Your Thoughts, Change Your Life*. It's something that I read every morning. It's about the many principles that promote mental wellness and having compassion for others—simply accepting others for who they are and not trying to change them. That's one of the major mistakes I've made over the years.

Is there anything that you would like to add that we haven't discussed so far?

I've gotten to a point in my life where I understand how important it is to help other people and avoid being selfish. I've got over a year of sobriety, and I try to cherish the time I have with friends and family. It's been a long, tough road for me. I'm so thankful for the support I've received from my close friends and family. I'm still working on navigating the many obstacles that life presents me every day. Working with the ERIC program and helping other people with bipolar is great therapy for me. Recently, helping autistic children within an equine therapy program in Colorado has taught me how lucky I am. In the end, it's all about giving back.

WHAT WORKS FOR GREG

- Quitting alcohol and illicit drugs
- Participating in support groups
- Reading inspirational books
- Practicing mindfulness and meditation
- Exercising regularly
- Receiving the support of family and friends

CHAPTER 10

MY STORY: HOW I BEAT DEPRESSION

AFTER MY FOURTH SUICIDE ATTEMPT, I spent about six weeks in the mental health unit at the Mayo hospital in Taree, which was about a forty-minute drive from my parents' home. Because I'd tried over twenty medications without much success, the clinical team decided to concentrate on psychological strategies. I had daily meetings with a psychologist who introduced me to the Buddhist concept of mindfulness. Mindfulness emphasizes the importance of living in the present. Its central message is that much psychological pain comes from dwelling on the past or being anxious about the future. The concept made sense, but I found it difficult to apply when I still had an overwhelming feeling of blackness within me. We decided to try stopping all medications to give my system a chance to clear out.

There was some improvement over my six-week stay, but it wasn't dramatic. I went back on medication, as the trial without any hadn't yielded results, and moved back in with my parents. But despite being on antidepressants again, I still had an overwhelming sense of dread and continued to feel suicidal.

The psychologist I'd been working with in the hospital moved on, and my sister Lyn, who was visiting from Sydney, helped me try to identify a suitable new therapist. It proved to be incredibly difficult in that rural location and required countless phone calls.

We ended up choosing a psychologist who visited from Sydney every two weeks. I saw him over the next few months, but I still had an overwhelming feeling of despair and darkness, along with an underlying anxiety that I couldn't seem to shake. The weeks kept rolling by. During that time my parents' support was unwavering, but I never felt like Forster was home. I was traveling to Sydney every two weeks to see my children. It was difficult seeing them so infrequently, and eventually I made the decision to move back to Sydney.

I moved into an apartment close to my children so I could see them more often. I also gradually began catching up with friends again. I started volunteering at Volunteering NSW, interviewing people and matching them with volunteer opportunities at nonprofit organizations. Earlier in my career I'd worked in recruitment, so this allowed me to use those skills for the greater good. This was beneficial, as it got me out of my head and helped me interact with other people. I also observed firsthand how working and volunteering boosted people's self-esteem.

BACK TO THE BRINK AGAIN

Even though I was functioning, my pessimistic outlook was still with me, and the feelings of anxiety returned and began to get worse. Without realizing it, I started the cycle of insomnia and fatigue again and got to the stage where I was absolutely desperate. I felt out of control. My psychiatrist, Dr. Fisher, decided that I should be booked into Northside Clinic, a psychiatric clinic in northern Sydney.

I spent nine weeks at Northside, once again trying some new medications, and also participating in group therapy. Because I didn't seem to be making any progress, I began a series of electroconvulsive therapy treatments, which caused real problems with my short-term memory.

After my time at Northside, my underlying anxiety was largely gone, but I still felt depressed. I felt well enough to leave, but far from strong and resilient. Back at home, I felt like I had too much time on my hands after the structured schedule at the clinic. I began an eight-week outpatient mood disorder program offered by the clinic. It was a group program facilitated by two psychologists and met two days a week. It was a relief having that regular commitment after the structured nature of a hospital stay.

The program mainly involved group therapy and also encouraged participants to set weekly goals in many realms of life: learning, recreation, spirituality, health, partner relationships, family, friends, and employment. We had to write our goals down and schedule when in the next week we would do them, and we knew we had to report back to the group the following week about whether we had followed through, which strengthened our commitment.

I found the goal setting extremely helpful. I'd done a lot of goal setting in business and in regard to my career, but I found that setting goals in all of these dimensions made me think more holistically about my life. It also gave me a sense of achievement when I could look back on my week and see that I'd done what I set out to do.

At about the same time, an old school friend reached out to me. She had been through similar mental health challenges and had a lot of empathy for what I was going through. We began a relationship, which eased my sense of loneliness and helped my self-esteem.

DISCOVERING WHAT I WANTED

Over time, it occurred to me that the three qualities I was seeking in life were vitality, intimacy, and prosperity (VIP). Vitality represented my personal health and well-being; intimacy was authenticity in relationships; and prosperity was my vocation and contribution to the world.

If you'd asked me before my breakdown if these qualities were important, I would have agreed without hesitation. What I saw in retrospect, however, was that if ever those three areas clashed, work (prosperity) usually won out over health and relationships. So I decided to make vitality my first priority, intimacy my second, and prosperity my third. I set weekly goals for myself in each area, and each Sunday I reviewed the goals I'd set the previous week and recorded my goals for the coming week.

The improvement in my mood was gradual, but it was definitely moving in the right direction. There were still mornings when I found it extremely difficult to get out of bed, but having short-term goals gave me a sense of purpose so that I could move despite those feelings.

CONSIDERING MEDICATION

I also continued to take the antidepressant medication prescribed by my psychiatrist, because I believed there was a biological element to my depression. I was so lucky to have Dr. Fisher. He always kept a level head, even when I was in crisis. I think the reassurance and hope he provided were of greater value than the medication.

It's hard to know the exact role that medication played in my recovery. It was crucial in the acute stage of my illness, and how it helped me get a good night's sleep was a godsend after spending so many nights staring at the ceiling. I'm not sure how much it contributed to lifting my mood. My thinking was far from sharp during that period, and I wasn't sure if that was due to my depression or the medication. Most likely it was a combination of the two. Antidepressants also had an adverse effect on my libido.

What I do know without doubt is that there's no way I would have had a sustained recovery if I'd relied solely on medication. The biggest frustration about medication is that it involves so much trial and error. After trying twenty-three different medications, my view is that they can ease symptoms, but they aren't the key to long-term well-being.

MY STRIVE2THRIVE ROADMAP

After many stumbles, much research, and a great deal of trial and error, about three years after I felt I was recovered I created a model to help me visualize how I would thrive. I call it the "Strive2Thrive Roadmap." I include it here to help you visualize the components that helped me get well.

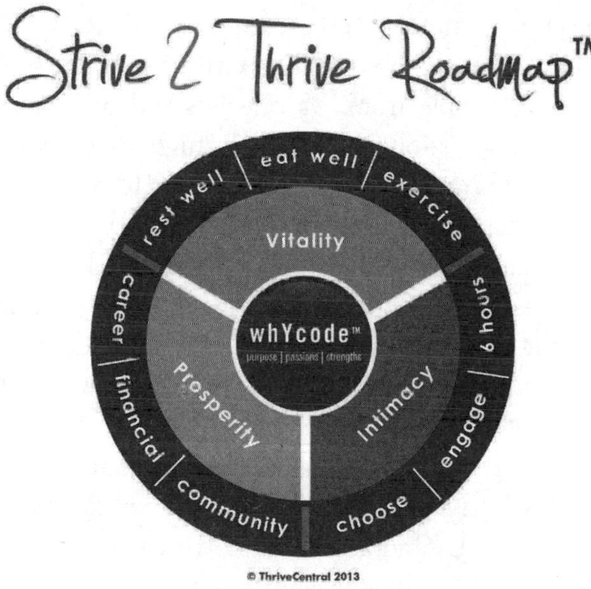

Vitality

In my model, vitality includes exercise, nutrition, meditation and spirituality, medication, recreation, fun, and sleep. Because this was my first priority, the first things I scheduled into my week were activities that promoted vitality. I decided that I'd walk for at least thirty minutes a day, six days a week. In the past I'd tried walking four days a week, but that didn't really transform the way I lived. As many of the interviews in this book reveal, and as you'll learn in chapter 11, many people find that exercise plays a major role in improving depression, yet it can be difficult to find the motivation to exercise when you're depressed. I'll provide some tips that should help with this in chapter 11.

I'm convinced that having daily rituals is the key to sustained behavior change, and evidence from *The Power of Full Engagement* (2005), by Jim Loehr and Tony Schwartz, confirms this. Now I begin each day with meditation and a walk. It's very centering and gets my day off to a great start.

At some point I stumbled across an article in *National Geographic* magazine that looked at three of the cultures with the greatest longevity, including people from Okinawa Island in Japan. All had very active lifestyles, along with a diet high in vegetables, fruit, nuts, and grains (85 percent), with some fish (10 percent), but only minimal amounts of meat, eggs, and dairy (Buettner 2005).

Some fascinating research by Felice Jacka and her colleagues at Deakin University in Melbourne (2011) found that it may be possible to prevent teenage depression by ensuring adolescents eat a sufficiently nutritious diet, and that improving diet may help treat depressive symptoms among teenagers. Jacka noted that three-quarters of lifetime psychiatric disorders emerge in adolescence or early adulthood, and that a recent UK survey indicated that more than 22 percent of UK adolescents age thirteen to eighteen had already experienced a clinically significant mental health problem.

Jacka's team found that a healthy diet predicted better mental health at follow-up. They defined a healthy diet as one that focuses on fruit and vegetables, including two or more servings of fruit per day and four or more servings of vegetables. In addition, an optimum diet generally excludes processed foods, including chips, fried foods, chocolate, sweets, and ice cream. It's gratifying that even in a conservative journal like *American Journal of Psychiatry*, an editorial in the March 2010 issue concluded, "It is both compelling and daunting to consider that dietary intervention at an individual or population level could reduce rates of psychiatric disorders" (Freeman 2010, 245).

Based on that *National Geographic* article, I changed my diet to include much more fruit, vegetables, and fish. I also began taking a fish oil supplement, as fish consumption has been linked to decreased incidence of depression (Hibbeln 1998). These dietary approaches, in combination with daily exercise, seemed to improve my energy levels. In addition, my mood slowly improved over a four-month period, from about 2 out of 10 to about 4 out of 10.

Resting well involves both sleep and the capacity to switch off. Getting a good night's sleep—a challenge for many who are depressed—is like hitting the reset button. From the standpoints of health, memory, appearance, and well-being, most people need seven to eight hours of sleep each night for optimal benefits (Rath and Harter 2010).

As I began to feel a little better, a friend told me about a meditation course she had done with the Brahma Kumaris, an India-based spiritual group that offers meditation instruction on a donation basis (see Resources). It was an eyes-open meditation that initially followed a guided commentary. I took a course and benefited greatly, so I now do the meditation twice a day, mornings and evenings, on most days. With continued practice, I started to experience a peace and self-love that I hadn't felt for a long time. I also began to feel that I had inner wisdom, and that the meditation helped me tap into it.

It's important to note that I'd tried meditation without much success when I was deeply depressed. I just didn't seem to be capable of experiencing the benefits. But the slightly improved mood that resulted from exercise seemed to make meditation practice easier. People often tell me that they've tried meditation and it doesn't work for them. I advise them to go to their local library and check out a few meditation CDs to see if a certain style of meditation might suit them. Like any new skill, it becomes easier with practice, and it's definitely worth investing in.

I also felt it was important to have some fun, so I started to play golf and go to the movies more regularly. As my health improved, I also began creating a Balinese-style garden and found that highly rewarding. Gardening helped me experience the present moment, and observing the growth of plants (or lack thereof) offered many metaphors for my own recovery.

In addition, as I began to approach my life more holistically, I found that my commitment to improving my physical and mental health allowed me to give more to my relationships.

Intimacy

In my model for recovery, I defined intimacy as honest, fun, and authentic interactions with my partner, family, close friends, work colleagues, and support group. I wanted to have authentic relationships—no more masks and Pollyannaish denial. I wanted to be as dedicated to my relationships with family and friends as I was to relationships in the workplace.

A 2009 poll of 140,000 people by the Gallup organization showed that those with the highest ratio of happiness to stress average six hours of social time each day (Rath and Harter 2010). That six hours includes time at work, at home, on the telephone, talking to friends, sending e-mail, social media, and so on. So I prioritized meeting and speaking with family and friends each week and tried to be more honest about how I was feeling. It's easier to be frank when you feel you're making progress, but even when I was having setbacks, I'd let a loved one know. When you've survived suicide attempts, it just doesn't seem appropriate to gloss over difficulties.

I also found myself far more tuned in to others' needs, and this helped me get out of my own head. I consider myself incredibly lucky to have a close and supportive family, and I know not everyone has that good fortune. If you don't have that emotional support,

I'll provide some recommendations on other sources of support in chapter 11.

I decided to reconnect with my mental health support group. The beauty of these groups is that you don't have to explain what depression is and how it impacts your life. Other group members have had similar issues, so their empathy is immediate and genuine, and members often support each other with phone contact between meetings. Eventually I took on the responsibility of organizing my local support group, which further increased my confidence. Providing there's sufficient trust, it's amazing how much people will share and help each other. In fact, many members of my group openly said that group support and accountability were the most important components of their recovery. (For further information about finding and choosing the right support group, see chapter 11.)

I was terrible at sharing my emotions, and I knew this had contributed to my difficulties in the past, but I felt I was making progress in this area. I attended a Pathways Foundation camp with my son—a program for fathers and their sons who are going through puberty. It borrows from the rite-of-passage rituals and ceremonies that are common in indigenous communities. It's a powerful experience that quickly builds trust and encourages participants to share their personal experiences. Many of the fathers commented that they had never experienced such honest sharing with other men.

I also began tracking down a few close friends I hadn't spoken to in years—even my best friend from when I was four. I was amazed at how quickly we rekindled the laughs and good times we'd shared at age four. Recently, I read Bronnie Ware's book *The Top Five Regrets of the Dying* (2012), which says that one of people's greatest regrets is not staying in touch with friends. I think men in particular let important friendships fall by the wayside when the treadmill of work, family, and life takes over. Placing a priority on important relationships also helped improve my self-esteem, and the more I gave, the more I received.

Many people gain considerable insight from meeting regularly with a counselor or therapist. As you'll learn in chapter 11, many of the people I surveyed found the emotional support and reassurance they received from their counselor essential to recovery, rating that as more important than the actual treatment they received.

Prosperity

The third element of my recovery road map is prosperity, and by that I mean a spirit of abundance rather than of scarcity. For me, this relates to career and my contribution to the world. The only way I could feel prosperous was to do something I thoroughly enjoyed and felt passionate about. During my career, I'd worked in sales and marketing and in human resources. Even though I'd enjoyed aspects of those roles, I believed the stress I had experienced from those roles contributed to my illness.

Having worked in recruitment and outplacement earlier in my career, I was convinced that an essential part of fulfilling work is identifying and building your strengths. The positive psychology movement, pioneered by Martin Seligman and popularized in his books *Authentic Happiness* (2002) and *Flourish* (2011), has contributed significantly to this approach. Among the twenty-four character strengths identified in positive psychology, my top five strengths are spirituality, curiosity, fairness, zest, and gratitude.

Marcus Buckingham and Tom Rath, from the Gallup Organization, have also written extensively about strengths in their books *StandOut* (Buckingham 2011) and *StrengthsFinder 2.0* (Rath 2007). My top five Gallup strengths are connectedness, developer, learner, maximizer, and positivity. Their assessments and language are more career focused than those of positive psychology, and both approaches are valuable. Knowing your strengths helps focus any exploration of career options.

Knowing my strengths, I explored becoming a business coach, but after researching this I realized that I had a stronger passion: to write a book on how people can overcome adversity and depression, based on the real-life experiences of others. I felt that this would give me a greater sense of purpose and help me put the skills I enjoy to work on a larger scale. I'm so thankful I decided to do it, because this is the most fulfilling work I've ever done.

As part of the spirit of abundance associated with prosperity, I also committed to donating at least 10 percent of my income or time to mental health advocacy groups.

Staying on the Path

I believe that deciding to live my life around these three priorities—vitality, intimacy, and prosperity—helped me focus on specific, positive outcomes, rather than just "I want to get over depression," and that this was significant in my recovery. Research into goal setting underscores that there is benefit in focusing on the positive (versus the negative). Setting weekly and longer-term goals in these categories gave me a sense of balance and purpose. (To download the planning form I use each week, go to http://www.iambackfromthebrink.com/thisweek.)

To reinforce my goals, I assembled pictures and other things that represented them, to paste in my notebook alongside them. For example, I had a mock-up cover of my book made, which helped it seem like a reality. I wanted to travel to Machu Picchu in Peru after I finished writing my book, so I added a picture of Machu Picchu.

When I experienced setbacks and disappointments, I found that the flat feeling that inevitably followed didn't last long. And the following week, when I'd write down my revised goals, I usually noticed that I was looking ahead rather than dwelling on the past. I want to stress that this sense of purpose and motivation didn't appear overnight. But as it grew, it also helped to gradually improve my self-esteem. And right from the start, I found it extremely beneficial to have weekly goals for my health, relationships, and work.

MY WHYCODE

The final part of my recovery was discovering what I call my whYcode. This is a combination of purpose, passions, and positive strengths. To move forward, I needed to decide three things:

- **Purpose:** My direction. Who am I going to serve, and how?
- **Passions:** My fuel. What motivates me and fires my spirit?
- **Strengths:** My tools. How can I use my strengths?

I almost hesitate to include this here as I believe it's hard to be definite about such things until you feel you're well on the way to recovery. Yet I do want to share it, because it may help you find meaning in your suffering and a compelling purpose—when the time is right. I recommend that you not spend too much time on this until your mood has improved enough that you're feeling hopeful, even if you still face many challenges related to your depression. Also, if you decide to use this planning tool, please be patient and flexible. It took a couple of years for me to eventually settle on the following purpose, passions, and strengths:

My Purpose

- Inspiring the discouraged to bounce back and thrive

My Passions

- Spending time in nature
- Practicing meditation
- Exercising
- Spending time with loved ones
- Enjoying music, photography, movies, travel, and cooking Asian food

My Strengths and How I Can Use Them

- Telling my story honestly, being grateful, and providing hope
- Seeing the big picture but also providing practical next steps
- Helping people identify their strengths and authentic self
- Seeing connections between disparate information and people
- Being curious and continually learning

I've developed a few other tools that can help you discover your passions and thrive. One is a questionnaire available at my website (www.iambackfromthebrink.com/whycode). But again, I'm acutely aware that it's much easier to talk about finding your purpose when you're feeling better and optimistic about the future. Another resource available at my website is a poster that summarizes the scientific research behind my approach (www.iambackfromthebrink.com/thriveposter). Ultimately, my hope is that the inspirational stories you've read in this book will encourage you to take action and find your own path to healing. Inactivity seldom defeats depression, whereas the right activities can provide a ladder out of the black hole.

GRATEFULNESS

One method that's very helpful in creating sustained improvements in well-being is writing down three things you're grateful for each day, perhaps at night before you go to bed. I know that forcing myself to write down three things I was grateful for each night, no matter how challenging my day had been, gradually changed how I saw the world.

This practice helped me see how very different my life is now. I have new priorities. Meditation helps me feel much calmer and more at peace with myself. Through my meditation, I now feel for the first time that I have a direct relationship with the Divine. I cherish my morning walks in the bush amidst nature. My relationships with my family and friends are closer and more rewarding. I love the creativity of my work and knowing that it may help others. I feel that everything I've done in the past is contributing to this work.

If you had told me when I was in the depths of depression that I'd be on this path and feeling so fulfilled, I wouldn't have believed you. Now I actually feel I'm a much better person for having gone through depression. I like myself. As extraordinary as it seems, I now view those five years of hell as a gift. If I hadn't been through that, I wouldn't have been forced to make changes in my priorities. I just wish I wasn't such a slow learner! I now know what strengthens me, and what weakens me. I'm more centered. I also spend much more time reflecting on what I have to be grateful for, rather than what I don't have.

One of the things I'm most grateful for is that, after twenty-two years of taking antidepressants, I am now off all medication. I'm not saying this is the right strategy for everyone. It was a decision I made after five years of good health, and in close consultation with my psychiatrist.

PAIN AS A PROMPT TO FIND MEANING

People often ask me what caused my depression. Looking back, there didn't appear to be any major triggers or crises, such as losing a spouse or long-term unemployment. I was diagnosed with melancholic depression, which is thought to be more biological in origin. However, I can see that most of my episodes were preceded by periods of stress. Looking back with the benefit of hindsight, I now believe that the root cause of my depression was having the wrong priorities in life. I believe that the core of my sustained recovery was identifying my purpose, passions, and strengths, and living by my whYcode. I'm also convinced that finding meaning in suffering is one of the most important elements of recovery, which is why I encourage people to discover their purpose (again, once overall mood has begun to improve). Personally, I found a remarkable opportunity to do this: helping establish Australia's R U OK? Day.

In 2009, I was approached by Gavin Larkin, an advertising CEO who had lost his father, Barry, to suicide fourteen years earlier. Barry had been the major influence in Gavin's life, and his death was devastating. Gavin felt like he was broken and could never be fixed. He also found himself in difficult conversations with his young children, who had never known their grandfather, trying to explain why Barry had taken his life. All of this fueled a passion to do work on suicide prevention.

Together with his friend Janina Nearn, a TV producer, Gavin created R U OK? Day (www.ruokday.com)—a day educating the general public about the importance of reaching out to people they're concerned about and asking, "Are you okay?"

I immediately embraced Gavin's vision because I knew from my own experience how important compassion and emotional support are to people in distress. The first R U OK? Day was six months away, and I threw myself into helping to make it a resounding success.

Those six months were a whirlwind of activity, and I dedicated hundreds of hours of volunteer work to the effort. Gavin worked for a large Australian communications organization, the STW Group, which included companies with expertise in website development, market research, public relations, lobbying, advertising, and social media marketing. Gavin persuaded STW's CEO, Mike Connaghan, to provide pro bono support, which was a critical element in our ultimate success.

Early highlights included all Australian mental health charities endorsing the day; News Corporation agreeing to provide editorial and advertising support; being launched at parliament by the federal health and aging minister; having Hugh Jackman, Naomi Watts, and Simon Baker provide video endorsements; creating a workplace program that hundreds of organizations participated in; having posters and resources delivered to five thousand doctors' offices; being endorsed by the prime minister; skywriting "RUOK" over Bondi Beach; and creating an extraordinary Facebook, Twitter, and YouTube campaign.

It was a roller-coaster ride with an extraordinary outcome, as millions of Australians participated in the day. The campaign has continued to grow in subsequent years. It's one of the most rewarding things I've ever been involved in, and it further fueled my recovery.

CHAPTER 11

DEPRESSION TREATMENTS THAT WORK

I BELIEVE THAT DEPRESSION RECOVERY RESEARCH IS too narrowly focused. The allocation of research funds is heavily biased toward areas where more money can be made, such as pharmaceuticals and counseling, with minimal attention to lifestyle and alternative approaches. In this chapter, I'll reveal what 4,064 people with mood disorders say worked best for them, and then outline an effective recovery plan.

LIMITATIONS OF CURRENT RESEARCH

At last count, Googling "depression" yields links to about 230 million pages, and Googling both "depression" and "treatments" turns up about 50 million pages. How on earth do you know where to start and what to believe?

In chapter 1, I tried to succinctly summarize the latest scientific research on the causes of depression and "evidence-based" treatments, based on the model used by Australia's Black Dog Institute. Most primary physicians recommend antidepressants, psychological counseling, or both. Yet despite huge increases in spending to treat depression, the World Health Organization (2001) reports that it's the most disabling illness in the West today, and that by 2020 it will be the second-most-disabling illness in the world. Why isn't the research into treating mood disorders producing better outcomes? Are researchers missing something?

David Freedman's book *Wrong: Why Experts Keep Failing Us—And How to Know When Not to Trust Them* (2010) highlights some surprising facts. It reveals the distorted ways in which some experts come up with advice, and why the most heavily flawed conclusions often get the most attention—all the more so in the online era. Freedman draws heavily on the work of John Ioannidis, a professor of medicine and director of the Stanford Prevention Research Center at Stanford University School of Medicine.

After sifting through hundreds of peer-reviewed medical studies published in highly respected journals, Ioannidis found that 66 percent were later proven to be wrong or had exaggerated results (Ioannidis 2005). The reasons for this are complex, so I encourage you to read Freedman's book or Ioannidis's article to learn more, but in brief, Freedman argues that we put too much faith in studies that purport to show more than they do. Studies, even the gold standard of research—random, double-blind, controlled studies—often have significant flaws that can and do lead us down the wrong path. And even though these flaws are known, they remain remarkably common. Freedman also highlights that both the way research is funded and the publication system sometimes lead scientists to push the boundaries about their claims.

I don't raise this issue to discredit scientists and mental health researchers. My wife, Karen Canfell, has a PhD from Oxford

University, and by any standard would be considered a global expert in her area of public health, though she is far too modest to claim this. I know how long and hard she works to ensure the rigor and validity of her work, and I've also seen her go to extreme lengths to avoid conflicts of interest and research bias. Unfortunately, a few researchers are not so rigorous, especially when there are conflicts of interest, as there often are in studies relating to pharmaceutical research findings, for example. Yet even if all research findings were correct, the persistence of the problem of depression underscores the question of whether researchers are missing something.

As I know all too well from my own experience, when people are depressed, they're ill-equipped to sort through mountains of often seemingly contradictory evidence regarding treatment effectiveness. You simply can't try all of the treatments that are advocated. And quite frankly, most depressed people struggle to simply get through the day. So who do you believe?

To further complicate the situation, doctors and counselors can be less than helpful when asked about the role of "alternative" treatments. Proponents of one approach often dismiss the benefits of others. For that matter, psychologists sometimes dismiss the role of medications, and psychiatrists underplay or don't even mention the benefits of psychological interventions, much less family support or exercise. They rely on the tools they're familiar with. Unfortunately, if you're holding a hammer, everything looks like a nail.

GOING TO THE SOURCE

Because of these limitations, I believe we need to develop a more holistic perspective to help guide decisions about treating depression and integrating medical and lifestyle approaches. When I started my first book, the Australian version of *Back from the Brink*, I decided to do some research of my own. I conducted a survey of people who had battled depression and bipolar disorder, and asked them what had worked best for them. Based on the 250 people who completed the survey, the eleven most effective strategies, starting with the most helpful, were as follows:

- Exercise
- Support of family and friends
- Counseling and therapy
- Fulfilling work
- Relaxation and meditation
- Nutrition
- Avoiding alcohol and drugs
- Prescription medications
- Support groups
- Religious and spiritual beliefs
- Contributing to a charity

As I was preparing to write this book, I decided that I'd do another survey, this time on a much larger scale. I wanted to explore even more factors, so I asked respondents to rate individual medications and specific psychological interventions. This approach wasn't intended to provide a definitive answer about which treatments are best; rather, the purpose was to establish broad themes to explore in a whole-person approach. The wording for the survey was adapted from a previous study and research paper by Professor Gordon Parker of the Black Dog Institute.

I asked respondents to rate the treatments they had tried and how much each had contributed to their recovery. (The options were *very effective*, *moderately effective*, *slightly effective*, *not effective*, *stopped before effectiveness could be judged*, and *didn't try*.) The following table shows the percentage of people who rated a treatment *very effective* or *moderately effective* from among those who tried that approach. Of the 4,064 people who completed the survey, 79.5 percent were from the United States and 70.4 percent were female. The number of respondents who tried each treatment is shown in parentheses.

Effectiveness of Depression Treatments	
Treatment	**Rated *very* or *moderately effective***
Psychiatrist—reassurance and support provided—questions regarding the specific treatments are asked separately (2,265)	64.3%
Psychologist—reassurance and support provided—questions regarding the specific treatments are asked separately (2,095)	60.8%
Support group and/or peer support (1,616)	59.3%
Vigorous exercise—the equivalent of running for 30 minutes 4–6 days per week (1,309)	58.3%
Other psychotherapy—involving a process whereby the therapist helps you explore and resolve issues related to past experiences and/or your personality style (1,727)	58.3%
Fulfilling work—paid or voluntary (2,190)	57.6%
Moderate exercise—the equivalent of walking for 30 minutes 4–6 days per week (2,129)	57.1%
Counseling—not about exploring unresolved themes, but a practical process, in which the counselor may take an educational approach; it involves you and the counselor discussing strategies for dealing better with day-to-day life (2,096)	57.1%

Treatment	Rated *very* or *moderately effective*
Emotional support from family and friends (2,533)	56.8%
A good night's sleep (2,617)	56.5%
Cognitive behavioral therapy (CBT)—focuses on changing negative thought patterns and usually involves doing structured homework tasks (1,642)	56.3%
ECT—electroconvulsive therapy or shock therapy (230)	56.1%
Reducing your intake of alcohol and other nonprescription drugs (1,682)	54.2%
Belief in God/spirituality/religion (2,099)	54.0%
Mindfulness-based cognitive therapy (MBCT), which includes simple breathing meditations and yoga stretches to help participants be more aware of the present and exercises from cognitive therapy that show links between thinking and feeling (1,170)	53.2%
Interpersonal/relationship psychotherapy (IPT), which focuses on improving interpersonal skills, conflict resolution, and relating to others generally (1,162)	52.8%
Acceptance and commitment therapy (ACT), one of the recent mindfulness-based therapies that combines Western psychology with Eastern philosophies (364)	52.7%
Hobbies, such as gardening, pets, or music (2,406)	51.2%
Massage (1,301)	49.8%
Yoga/meditation (1,320)	49.3%
Being able to let go of unrealistic goals (1,860)	47.7%

Treatment	Rated *very* or *moderately effective*
Quetiapine, brand name Seroquel (897)	47.6%
Relaxation (2,160)	44.6%
Good nutrition—a diet high in fruit and vegetables and lean protein, and low in saturated fats and processed sugars (2,047)	43.8%
Aripiprazole, brand name Abilify (695)	43.2%
Venlafaxine, brand name Effexor (1,171)	41.7%
Duloxetine, brand name Cymbalta (681)	40.8%
Bupropion, brand name Wellbutrin, Zyban, or Aplenzin (1,319)	40.8%
Keeping a gratitude journal to record what you are grateful for on a regular basis (1,036)	39.8%
Acupuncture (417)	38.9%
Olanzapine, brand name Zyprexa (474)	37.6%
Fluoxetine, brand name Prozac (1,255)	37.4%
Risperidone, brand name Risperdal (539)	34.5%
Tranylcypromine, brand name Parnate (89)	34.4%

Themes

The results demonstrate that no one treatment is clearly superior, and that to recover as quickly as possible, it's a good idea to consider a multipronged approach. Five major themes emerged:

- Emotional support or compassion
- Psychological treatments

- Lifestyle strategies
- Fulfilling work
- Prescription medications

EMOTIONAL SUPPORT

Emotional support, reassurance, and compassion from psychiatrists, psychologists, support groups, and family and friends dominate the top ten most effective strategies. These results emphasize what social creatures we are and how we crave empathy and connection. It's fascinating that the emotional support and reassurance psychiatrists and psychologists provide is judged to be more important than their treatments. This supports the scientific literature indicating that the quality of the relationship between clinician and patient is the best predictor of a successful outcome (Martin et al. 2005). I know that during my horrendous five-year depressive episode, the reassurance and support of my psychiatrist, Dr. Fisher, was paramount. Even though I remained depressed after trying twenty-three different medications, I never blamed him or questioned his competence.

This finding highlights the importance of having a good relationship with your clinician. If you don't, or if you don't feel confident about the clinician's treatment plan, find someone else to work with. How technically brilliant your doctor or therapist is doesn't really matter if you don't have strong rapport and trust.

PSYCHOLOGICAL TREATMENTS

Other psychological treatments, including psychoanalysis, counseling, cognitive behavioral therapy, mindfulness-based cognitive therapy, interpersonal therapy, acceptance and commitment therapy, and letting go of unrealistic goals were all rated highly. For more details on many of these therapeutic approaches, review chapter 1.

LIFESTYLE STRATEGIES

Exercise, whether vigorous or moderate, was rated as very effective. Other highly rated lifestyle approaches include getting a good night's sleep, being able to relax, doing meditation or yoga, engaging in hobbies, getting massages, and reducing intake of alcohol and recreational drugs.

FULFILLING WORK

It is fascinating that fulfilling work is rated more highly than cognitive behavioral therapy, which is often considered a highly effective depression treatment. Having worked in recruitment, outplacement, and career management for fifteen years, I experienced firsthand how few people work in roles that allow them to use their strengths and feel that they're doing something meaningful. The Gallup Organization found that only 20 percent of employees give a strong yes to "Do you like what you do each day?" (Rath and Harter 2010). Furthermore, they found that people with high career well-being were more than twice as likely to be thriving in their life overall.

I personally experienced the benefits of doing voluntary work in my own recovery. My voluntary work involved placing discouraged people (new migrants or people rehabilitating from physical or mental illness) into volunteer positions with charities. I saw how the work lifted their self-esteem and confidence. Unfortunately, not many mental health professionals have the experience to provide insightful career advice.

PRESCRIPTION MEDICATIONS

Most people who see their primary physicians because of depressive symptoms are prescribed antidepressants. However, the results of my survey indicate that relying on medication as a sole strategy to overcome depression is unwise. While medication can play an invaluable role in recovery from depression, its curative properties have been heavily oversold. One frustration with medication is that a certain drug can be highly effective for one person, but ineffective or even harmful for another. This reinforces the importance of working with a doctor who's highly experienced in successfully treating mood disorders.

Using These Results

After listening to 4,064 fellow travelers, I identified four key issues people with depression need to consider:

- How to build a network that provides more compassion and emotional support
- How to access great mental health professionals
- How to find fulfilling work
- How to incorporate exercise and other health-supporting behaviors into daily life

CREATING A RECOVERY PLAN THAT WORKS

For those of us who live with a predisposition to depression, inertia is the greatest enemy. When you're depressed, it seems perfectly natural to believe that nothing will help. I know that was true for me. Furthermore, I didn't even ask for help because I was ashamed to admit that I wasn't coping. This feeling is common, especially for men, who have often been socialized to be problem solvers and self-sufficient. Every week, I hear from women who are desperately trying to get husbands, boyfriends, brothers, or fathers to admit they have a problem and need help.

What I learned after five episodes of major depression (unfortunately, I seem to be a very slow learner) is that taking action is essential to recovery. As highlighted earlier, there's rarely a single silver bullet. When starting the journey toward recovery, a multistrategy approach is wisest because you can't know which treatments will be most effective for you. To encapsulate the four key issues outlined above, I created the acronym CARE. It will help you come up with an approach that covers all of the bases in effective self-care:

C Compassion and building emotional support

A Accessing great mental health experts

R Revitalizing work

E Exercising daily

Assessing Mood

Before I discuss specific recommendations in these four areas, let's take a look at mood and assessing mood. This is obviously a key topic, as people who are depressed yearn for a sustained improvement in mood. Having a way of assessing your mood, and using that technique over time, is a key way to chart your progress. Seeing your progress will help you know which strategies work best for you; it will also be heartening and can fuel your recovery.

Every time I visited my psychiatrist, he inevitably asked me to rate my mood from 0 to 10. Having learned how important these ratings are, I developed the moodometer below (inspired by the Resilience and Wellbeing Thermometer developed by Mental Health at Work, www.mhatwork.com.au).

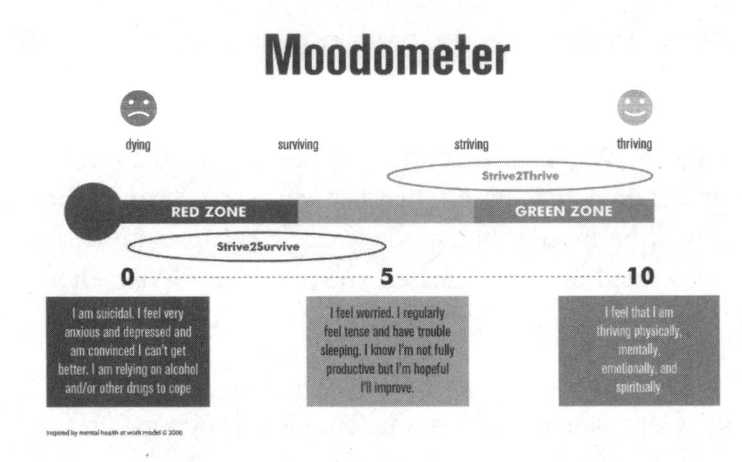

The rating of 5 on this scale is critical, because at 5 you can remember having been well in the past, whereas at lower ratings you usually can't. This chapter is primarily written for those whose mood is between 0 and 6.

Before I delve into recommendations on creating an effective treatment plan, one last thought on mood. In her book *The How of Happiness* (2008), Sonja Lyubomirsky, a professor of psychology at the University of California, Riverside, writes that well-being is a function of genetics (50 percent), circumstances (10 percent), and the actions we take (40 percent). She concludes that because we can't change our genetic makeup and often can't control events, the only area where we have absolute control is our actions—how we respond to life circumstances. Keep this in mind as you create your own recovery plan. And now let's turn to the four elements of CARE: compassion and emotional support, access to great mental health professionals, revitalizing work, and exercising daily.

Compassion and Building Emotional Support

Suffering in silence doesn't work. Although you may think you're rational, the more depressed you are, the more divorced from reality your thinking is. When I attempted to take my own life, I was 100 percent convinced that I would never get better. I couldn't have been more wrong. In contrast, my parents, who I was living with at the time, could remember me when I was well and were in a much better position to observe changes in my mood objectively. The value of compassionate support, whether from family, friends, other loved ones, support groups, or coworkers, can't be overstated.

Sadly, depressed people often want to isolate themselves and push others away due to feelings of shame. I urge you to resist that inclination. One of the greatest factors preventing depressed people from asking for help and admitting that they aren't coping is the perception that others' opinions of them will decline if they admit to feeling hopeless. In a survey of 2,676 people living with depression or bipolar disorder, I asked whether they had personally experienced stigma because of their mood disorder. Sadly, 41 percent strongly agreed, 24 percent moderately agreed, 18 percent slightly agreed, 8 percent disagreed, and 8 percent said the issue wasn't relevant. In total, 83 percent felt they had experienced stigma.

To understand more about the source of that stigma, I asked who they felt comfortable talking with about their depression or bipolar disorder. The results are presented in the following table.

I feel comfortable discussing my depression (or bipolar disorder) with...		
	Very or moderately comfortable	Not relevant
My partner or spouse	49%	27%
My friends	47%	3%
Members of my family	49%	3%
My work colleagues	14%	18%
My primary care physician or general practitioner	66%	5%

Not surprisingly, many people feel most comfortable talking with their doctor about their illness, which stresses the need for a relationship where empathy and trust are prevalent (more on that topic later).

Even though you may not be comfortable discussing how you're feeling with those closest to you, you're likely to find that your loved ones have noticed changes in your mood and demeanor and would like to help. I recommend that you be kind to yourself and confide in those you trust and respect. Keeping your thoughts to yourself when you're depressed tends to be harmful. Unfortunately, when you're depressed you don't have an accurate perception of reality, so you may be overly pessimistic about your situation.

At my seminars, people often say that they don't have anyone who understands or cares about their despair. Although this often isn't the case, later I will discuss strategies for people who hold this belief.

Talking with others is one of the best things you can do if you're depressed. Maintaining a support system is incredibly helpful for recovery. There are three main categories of people you can build emotional support with:

- Loved ones, such as a spouse or partner, family members, or close friends

- Support groups
- Coworkers and employee assistance programs

LOVED ONES

As my survey on stigma indicated, many people don't feel comfortable discussing their depression with their spouse, family, or friends. However, most people do have at least one person they can confide in, and that's a start. A problem shared is a problem halved. When opening such a dialogue, choose a private place and a situation where you can both speak freely. I feel that these conversations are often most effective when two people are walking in nature and not necessarily looking directly at each other. Here are some pointers on how to approach the discussion.

It's okay to say you're not coping or have lost hope. With depression, feelings of despair often come with the territory. It's important that people understand you aren't having an ordinary "down day" or "down week." Be honest. Don't be afraid to say exactly what you're feeling and explain that you can't snap out of it. Also let the other person know which strategies you've tried so far.

Start by describing what you're experiencing. When you're depressed, it feels like everything is wrong and the situation will never improve. Still, try to be specific. What are the major factors causing your despondency? It can be hard to put your finger on one thing or just a few things, but try. Is there one major stressor or a combination of things you can be specific about? Tell the other person about your symptoms, whether they include early morning waking, anger, loss of appetite, low energy levels, black thoughts, zero self-esteem, or lost libido.

Don't be afraid to ask for help. Many people, particularly men, find it difficult to admit that they can't solve the situation on their own. Admitting to yourself and others that you need help is an essential part of moving forward. The first step in any 12-step program is admitting that you can't fix things yourself. In my experience, the vast majority of people react with genuine compassion when a loved one asks for help. In fact, a common frustration among caregivers is that their loved one, who is obviously struggling, won't ask for or seek help.

Suggest that others learn about the illness and treatments. If others ask how they can help, mention that it would be beneficial for them to learn more about the different types of depression and treatments. Suggest that they read chapters 1 and 11 of this book. If they don't ask how they can help, suggest this strategy anyway. Also encourage them to read some of the interviews in this book.

Ask for help in finding great mental health professionals. In my research, the greatest regret of most depressed people is not seeking expert help or a diagnosis earlier. A bit later in this chapter, I'll offer pointers on how to find effective mental health professionals.

Ask to meet for a regular walk. As highlighted previously, when you're depressed, going for a walk may be the last thing you feel like doing; however, the benefits are undeniable. You're much more likely to walk if you have a commitment to walk with a loved one. Ask loved ones to encourage you to exercise regularly, and explain that it isn't easy to do when you're depressed.

ALTERNATIVES TO SUPPORT FROM LOVED ONES

Many people have told me that they don't have loved ones to support them. Regretfully, this is true for some people. But even in this situation, you still have some options: support groups (discussed next), pets, and organizations that can connect you with people who provide emotional support.

Compeer (www.compeer.org) is one such organization. They train volunteers to provide support to people living with mental health challenges and their families. Volunteers are encouraged to make weekly contact either by phone or by meeting up for outings.

They operate in the United States and Australia, and work toward social inclusion, community integration, and natural support systems. A friend of mine volunteers and speaks highly of the benefits to both her new friend and herself. Similar support is often available through churches and community groups. Your doctor may be able to point you toward such an organization.

Many people derive extraordinary emotional support from a pet. Some people I've talked with have insisted that this was the most important component of their recovery and were effusive about the unconditional love they received. In addition, the responsibility of taking care of another being can be a welcome change from the self-obsession that often accompanies depression. As a bonus, if your pet is a dog, you'll probably have to take it for a walk each day, which will also be beneficial for you.

SUPPORT GROUPS

As indicated by my surveys, people who have been depressed give high ratings to support groups as a treatment strategy. Some support groups are more general, whereas others are specific to a particular disorder or population. In this section I'll give you some pointers about finding a group that's a good fit for you, but first I'd like to share my own experience with support groups.

I helped run Bounce, a support group for people with mood disorders, for eight years. Our group met for two hours each week and was run by members. It followed a structure that allowed time for status reports and problem solving for each member. Members were encouraged to bring up issues they were having and solutions they were considering. The group would then offer input on those or other options. Based on that input, the person was asked to choose a practical task to undertake during the next week to address the issue. Another group member was assigned to follow up during the week to check on progress and provide support.

The program included a component of challenging irrational thoughts, so it was quite congruent with the principles of cognitive behavioral therapy. In addition, we set aside time to read and discuss interesting articles and studies on well-being, and members were encouraged to call each other between meetings to check in.

The main benefit members reported was meeting people who really understood what they were experiencing. As a result, they didn't feel so alone. It wasn't uncommon for new members to bring a partner, parent, or friend along to their first meeting to give them moral support. If they chose to continue attending, we asked that they come by themselves and take responsibility for their own recovery. We also suggested that they attend for at least three meetings before deciding whether to join the group, because it's difficult to get a good feel for how it works in just one or two visits.

I've witnessed many recoveries through Bounce, and definitely encourage you to consider a support group. Many of the people in our group also saw a psychiatrist, psychologist, or both, but they tended to say that the emotional support and insight they received from the group was the most important element in their recovery.

However, this isn't true for everyone. The support group model works better for some than for others. Plus, not all support groups are the same, and aside from different orientations or focal points, each also has a unique culture depending on the leaders and members. I tried a couple of others before finding Bounce, and they just weren't right for me. I highly recommend that you find a support group that works well for you. If you choose to, here are some things to consider:

General or specific focus. Some groups are open to all people with a mental illness, whereas others focus on specific problems, such as depression or bipolar disorder. There is no reason you can't be involved with two groups if you find both helpful.

Meeting style. Are you more likely to benefit from a formal, structured meeting, or do you prefer to hang out and chat? Pick a group that follows a format you're likely to feel comfortable with. Whatever the style of the group, please bear in mind that what's discussed in the group stays in the group.

Longevity and leadership. Look for a group that has some longevity but is still able to attract new members. Ideally, a group will have a good mix of regulars and newer members. More experienced members can speak with credibility about recovery, while newer members keep the group from getting stuck in a rut. Also look for a group leader who's inclusive and compassionate but also challenging. A support group isn't the place to indulge in theories. To be effective, a leader needs to have some personal experience with depression or at least a thorough understanding of the difficulties people with mood disorders face.

Your goals. Be clear about what a support group provides. These groups aren't a form of therapy. The purpose of a support group is to help its members deal with issues related to their disorder. If you find that you've got more on your mind than you think is appropriate for the group, talk to your health care professional. If you don't have a doctor or therapist, you can ask the group for recommendations. Also, be aware that a support group shouldn't just be a lovefest. Although friendship and emotional support are essential elements, neither one is the primary aim. The primary aim is to get well, and for that to happen, a good support group must sometimes be challenging, taking everyone a bit outside their comfort zone and collectively holding members accountable. If you don't do something different, things will stay the same.

Many mental health organizations offer support groups or can recommend groups in your area. The Depression and Bipolar Support Alliance (www.dbsalliance.org) and the National Alliance on Mental Illness (www.nami.org) both have an extensive network of groups throughout the United States. Your doctor or therapist may also be able to recommend support groups.

WORKPLACE SUPPORT

Career well-being is an essential element of overall well-being. It's better to continue working while you're receiving treatment if you can, rather than sit at home and watch the walls. However, there is still extraordinary stigma in the workplace regarding mental illness. As outlined above, only 14 percent of the people I surveyed about stigma felt comfortable discussing their mood disorders with colleagues.

I was once asked by the Black Dog Institute to be a judge in a writing competition where people described what it's like to live with a mood disorder in the workplace. Reading those two hundred essays revealed that many people are uncomfortable disclosing their depression at work because they fear this could compromise their career prospects. Many organizations have a strongly performance-driven culture that supports this belief.

Because I've told my story so publicly, most people feel comfortable telling me their own story or that of someone close to them with a mood disorder. I speak extensively to corporate groups, and in every presentation I ask people to raise their hands if they're close to someone with depression or a mood disorder. Without fail, 70 to 90 percent of the people in the audience raise their hands. So although people always feel alone when experiencing a mood disorder, these difficulties are very common.

I encourage you to find someone in your workplace you can confide in, if at all possible. It can be anyone—a team member, a manager, someone in HR or another department—but try to choose someone who's compassionate and who knows the personalities and culture of the organization. In your communications, follow the principles for talking with loved ones outlined above. Ask this person whether he or she is close to anyone who has experienced depression, and whether he or she would be willing to support you while you're struggling.

Also ask for advice on whether it would be prudent to discuss your situation with your manager. This is the best approach if the company and your manager have the right values. Although the Americans with Disabilities Act stipulates that an organization can't discriminate against people who have a mental illness, I know people who feel they've been discriminated against after disclosing their illness. This can reflect the values of an individual manager or of the organization as a whole.

That said, telling your manager what's happening can be helpful when you need time off to see a therapist or doctor. It will also help your manager understand that there are sound reasons for any changes in your productivity. Let your intuition—and that of a coworker you trust—be your guide as to how widely you discuss your situation.

Many larger organizations provide access to employee assistance programs (EAPs), which offer confidential advice to employees about personal and family difficulties. Many programs can facilitate a certain number of free confidential sessions with a qualified therapist. If an employee assistance program is available to you, it can probably provide advice on how you can build emotional support for yourself within the organization. The organization you work for won't know you consulted the employee assistance program; while they receive statistics from the program, they do not have access to any identifying data. Check with human resources or your company's intranet to see if this service is available to you.

Accessing Great Mental Health Experts

As mentioned, people who have been through a severe bout of depression (and their loved ones) often tell me that if they had it to do over, they would seek expert help much earlier. If you haven't yet done so, you may wonder how to find a qualified professional with expertise in depression or bipolar disorder.

The key players in a mental health team usually include a primary care physician, psychologist, and psychiatrist, and possibly a social worker, exercise physiologist, or other type of therapist. In the long run, you need to have solid relationships with everyone on your team—but first you have to assemble your team. To do so, seek referrals from people you trust:

- **Family and friends.** If a loved one has had a positive experience with a mental health professional, ask him or her about the experience to see if the same doctor might be right for you. It's no guarantee, but since your loved one knows both of you, he or she is in a better position to make an assessment.

- **Other respected associates.** Other people that you know well and trust, such as your lawyer, accountant, or religious leader, may be able to provide recommendations.

- **Your managed care provider or insurer.** Many insurance companies rate their providers, and some even reimburse at higher rates for the top-ranked professionals. Ask whether your program does this.

- **Your employee assistance program.** Many large employers provide free professional psychological support to their employees through employee assistance programs. If one is available, seek advice on care providers.

- **Other care providers.** If you're happy with one care provider, such as your psychologist, and now need a psychiatrist or primary care physician, ask that care provider for a recommendation.

PRIMARY CARE PHYSICIANS

Alarmingly, during doctors' initial college education, most institutions devote little attention to depression, anxiety, and other mental illnesses. Plus, primary care physicians (PCPs) have a huge number of specialty areas to cover, and many choose to focus solely on physical health. However, many PCPs do say that the root cause of patients' problems is often a mood disorder.

If you're struggling emotionally, the importance of having a well-trained, caring PCP quickly becomes evident. A good PCP can be a linchpin, integrating care from specialists such as psychologists and psychiatrists. Seek a PCP who's a good listener, who cares, and who communicates in language you understand. Your PCP should have relevant expertise and intellectual curiosity, and should also be comfortable recommending lifestyle approaches and other holistic interventions, such as massage or acupuncture. Finally, a good PCP will be comfortable admitting when he or she doesn't have sufficient expertise to provide the right answer and will be able to refer you to a competent specialist.

When first meeting with a PCP to discuss your depression (or any other mental health issue), there are a few things you can do to maximize your chances of getting an accurate diagnosis and appropriate treatment plan. They will also help the PCP to determine if he or she can meet all of your care needs or whether you also need to consult with a psychologist or psychiatrist.

First, advise the receptionist that you'd like to book a long consultation to discuss a mental health issue. If this isn't a possibility, it's unlikely that the practice is the right one for you.

Then, prepare to describe your situation as succinctly as possible. You might want to jot down a few notes. Here are some pointers on the types of information you'll need to share:

- The symptoms you've been experiencing
- How long you've had those symptoms
- The extent to which your symptoms impact your home and work life
- Any triggers, such as stressful events
- The level of emotional support available to you
- Any family history of depression or mental illness
- Whether you're attempting to self-medicate with alcohol or drugs
- Whether you're suicidal

Finally, you might want to take a loved one with you. In addition to providing emotional support, your loved one may be able to take notes and provide additional information or help you keep track of the PCP's assessment and recommendations.

Afterward, assess the visit and the suitability of the PCP by asking yourself the following questions:

- Did the PCP care?
- Did the PCP ask the right questions to understand my situation?
- Did the PCP propose a preliminary diagnosis and outline a holistic treatment plan (for example, not relying solely on antidepressants) that I have confidence in?

If you can't answer yes to all three questions, you may wish to explore other options.

PSYCHOLOGISTS

Psychologists are trained to help people cope with emotional problems and lead a more fulfilling life. In addition to providing counseling or talk therapy, they may utilize specific treatments or approaches depending on the client's diagnosis. For descriptions of the types of psychotherapy best suited to treating depression or bipolar disorder, see chapter 1. Most psychologists don't undertake medical training. Therefore, they generally aren't qualified to prescribe medication, and in most US states, they are prohibited from doing so.

As with visiting a PCP for a mental health issue, before meeting with a psychologist for the first time, prepare to describe your situation as succinctly as possible by jotting down some notes about your symptoms and so on, as outlined above.

I recommend viewing your first visit as a test-drive. Try to determine whether you think you can build a strong, trusting relationship with this person. After the first visit, consider these questions:

- Did the session feel worthwhile?
- Did the psychologist understand your situation?
- Did the psychologist seem genuinely interested in helping?
- Did the psychologist outline a plan you had confidence in?
- Do you trust the psychologist and want to return?

If you don't feel comfortable with one psychologist, keep looking. As mentioned, most people find that the emotional support and reassurance they receive from a psychologist is more important than the actual treatment strategy. If you feel you won't receive this from a psychologist, you'll be missing an essential element.

PSYCHIATRISTS

Psychiatrists train as medical doctors first and then go on to train in psychological medicine—using medication as a treatment strategy. They are also trained in talk therapies, but many of them focus on medication. (Some psychiatrists do place greater emphasis on talk therapy and alternative approaches, but they tend to be harder to find.) Because many people benefit from medication, there are huge advantages to working with a psychiatrist who specializes in the mental health problem you're struggling with.

Some people are reluctant to try medication because they've heard negative reports about it. While it isn't wise to rely solely on medication as a treatment, some people have tried everything else to no avail, only to discover that pharmaceuticals really helped. For some conditions, such as bipolar disorder and melancholic and psychotic depression, medication is often essential. However, medication is not an exact science (as I well know, having tried twenty-three different kinds), so even if the first medication you try doesn't work, keep trying.

Preparing to see a psychiatrist is much the same as preparing to see a PCP. If you've already tried medication, the psychiatrist will want to know which ones you've used, the dosages, if you experienced any benefits or side effects, and why you discontinued any medication for your mood.

Again, there are advantages to having a loved one attend the first session if you're comfortable with this. It can be hard to remember the names of various drugs and their benefits and side effects when you aren't well and your memory is impaired.

Revitalizing Work

In their book *Wellbeing* (2010), Tom Rath and Jim Harter identify five essential elements for a thriving life: career well-being, social well-being, financial well-being, physical well-being, and community well-being. Their findings are based on research by the Gallup Organization, which conducted a comprehensive study in 150 countries to understand what qualities lead to sustainable well-being. Rath and Harter analyzed the information and found that while 66 percent of people are thriving in one of the five areas, only 7 percent are thriving in all of them. And, while each of the five elements is important, their analysis concluded that career well-being was arguably the most critical. People with high career well-being were twice as likely to be thriving in their lives overall.

My fifteen years of experience in recruitment, outplacement, and career management fully confirm this finding, and my surveys have shown similar results, with fulfilling work being highly rated as a strategy for overcoming depression. In addition, a surprising study published in the *Economic Journal* showed that for men, a year's unemployment may be the one adverse event they don't fully recover from after five years—even worse than the death of a spouse (Clarke et al. 2008).

As mentioned, an important component of my own recovery was volunteer work that involved connecting people recovering from physical and mental disabilities with volunteer positions. Suddenly they had a reason to get out of bed each day, interact with other people, and make a contribution, instead of being idle at home. The lift in their confidence, even after just one month, was remarkable.

I define revitalizing work as utilizing your inherent strengths to serve others. I'm not saying you should try to find your career calling when you're severely depressed—that's entirely unrealistic. But taking on a role that helps boost your self-esteem can start you on a journey. I never dreamed that my volunteer work would lead me to write books and speak at conferences.

Because finding revitalizing work is a huge topic that could fill an entire book, here I'll limit the discussion to two key topics: identifying your strengths, and figuring out how you can use them to help others.

IDENTIFYING YOUR STRENGTHS

As mentioned, several resources can be extremely useful in discovering and understanding your strengths: positive psychology, the Clifton StrengthsFinder, and the MAPP Test.

In 1998, Martin Seligman, one of the main founders of positive psychology and president of the American Psychological Association, observed that, for too long, psychology had been obsessed with what was wrong with people and decided that he wanted to devote more time to what was right. This led to the birth of positive psychology and eventually the book *Authentic Happiness* (Seligman 2002). Seligman and his colleague Christopher Pearson developed a list of character strengths and virtues based on research into cultures across the globe and across millennia—from ancient China and India, through Greece and Rome, to contemporary Western cultures. They identified twenty-four character strengths, and created a research questionnaire to help people identify their top five strengths. You can complete this free assessment at Martin Seligman's Authentic Happiness website (www.authentichappiness.org).

The Gallup Organization, founded in 1935, was initially involved in independent polling. In 1999, using more than thirty years of in-depth research, Gallup scientists led by Donald O. Clifton, PhD, created one of the first career assessment tools and training programs based on what is *right* with people. This program is built on the Clifton StrengthsFinder, a web-based talent assessment tool. As of this writing, more than 8.6 million people worldwide have taken the Clifton StrengthsFinder assessment. For a small fee, you can take the assessment online (www.gallupstrengthscenter.com) to discover your top five strengths. Or, if you purchase the book *StrengthsFinder 2.0* (Rath 2007), the online assessment is free.

The Gallup Organization has shown that people who use and build their strengths on a weekly basis are six times more likely to be engaged in their jobs and three times more likely to report having an excellent quality of life than those who don't (Rath 2007). I completed and used both Seligman's survey and the Gallup assessment as part of my recovery and found both extremely valuable. There is, of course, some overlap in their findings, and also some subtle differences. For example, the positive psychology assessment is more applicable to life as a whole, whereas the Gallup assessment is more directly related to workplace strengths.

You might also be interested in an online assessment called the Motivational Appraisal of Personal Potential (MAPP). Although some results are available at no cost, to receive useful detailed information, you must pay a fee. According to the MAPP website (www.assessment.com), over 7 million people have completed the MAPP career questionnaire. What I like about this profile is that, in addition to identifying your abilities, it informs you which professions you're ideally suited for, and also provides information on qualifications for each career. I completed this profile a number of years ago, and my career now exactly reflects its recommendations.

WHO DO YOU WISH TO SERVE?

Whether you're a volunteer or paid for your work, it's preferable to be in an organization whose mission provides a clear sense of purpose that's congruent with your values. If you believe in the organization's purpose, it's more likely that the work will energize you. As I was coming out of my black hole, I asked myself how I could use that horrific episode to serve others. That was the sense of purpose that motivated me when I didn't feel like getting out of bed. It's also helpful to be involved in an organization that truly values people and that has clients you like.

Exercising Daily

Nobody doubts the benefits of exercise for physical health. What isn't as widely discussed is how essential moderate exercise is to mental well-being. In the surveys I conducted, exercise received extraordinarily high ratings as a strategy for overcoming depression. Research shows that a twenty-minute brisk walk or the equivalent significantly improves mood for two, four, eight, and even twelve hours later (Mayo Clinic 2008). Exercise also boosts energy, confidence, and perception of sexual desirability (Krucoff and Krucoff 2000). You can't control the slings and arrows that come your way on a daily basis, but you can control your daily habits. Incorporating moderate exercise into your day can decrease your chances of a prolonged setback.

People typically give two main reasons for not exercising. One is that they don't feel like it. This is particularly applicable to people who are discouraged, depressed, or both. The other is not having time. The relentless pace of modern life usually means there are a thousand things to say yes to. However, an essential element of a thriving life is saying no to the trivial many so you can say yes to the vital few. Exercise is definitely in the latter category. Given how common these attitudes are, here are a few pointers on how you can make exercise central to your life.

FIND SOMETHING YOU ENJOY

To sustain an exercise program, it's important to do something that you enjoy. The traffic in gyms is 30 to 50 percent higher in

January than other times of the year. New Year's resolutions inspire people to get fit and lose weight, but by March, attendance levels have returned to normal. The not-so-hidden message here is that it isn't wise to sign up for activities that you don't like.

The key is to choose activities that you like and will engage in over the long term, whether swimming, dancing, cycling, boot camps, or hiring a personal trainer. To experience mood enhancement benefits, most people need at least thirty minutes of exercise six days per week. Although people with depression often don't feel like exercising, it's important to fight that inclination. I enjoy walking because it allows me to get out in nature, it's free, and I can do it anytime, anywhere. You might enjoy keeping a walking journal to record what you see, hear, smell, and feel each day, to help keep you present.

HAVE MODEST GOALS

Many people believe that to get the benefits of exercise you have to spend two hours in the gym or run a marathon. As highlighted above, this simply isn't true. If you haven't been exercising, start with fifteen minutes per day. If you're spending all day in bed, just walking for ten minutes each day is a good start that you can build on gradually.

CREATE RITUALS

Changing behavior requires more than intention. To make it stick, you need to create daily rituals that prompt the new behavior. Here are some examples of rituals that can support regular exercise:

- If you exercise in the morning, lay out your exercise clothes at night when you go to bed so you can get ready more easily in the morning.

- As you brush your teeth each morning, put on a pedometer. When you brush at night, take it off and record how many steps you took. Start by just monitoring your steps for the first week, and then build the average daily count by 10 percent each week until you get to ten thousand steps per day—a level of exercise associated with numerous benefits (Morgan, Tobar, and Snyder 2010).
- Set a regular time to walk with a friend or colleague. If walking with coworkers, consider walking meetings. This kills two birds with one stone.
- Consider using a free smartphone app like MyFitnessPal, which allows you to monitor your exercise and calorie consumption.

TIPS ON TAKING ACTION

So, how do you extend CARE (compassion, accessing great mental health experts, revitalizing work, and exercise) to yourself when you don't like yourself and have no energy? As mentioned at the beginning of this chapter, 40 percent of our well-being is determined by our daily actions (Lyubomirsky 2008), so the importance of taking action in these four areas cannot be underestimated. Even if you don't feel like it, "fake it until you make it," as the saying goes. I know all too well that this isn't easy when your natural instinct is to do nothing. However, the following strategies can be enormously helpful in making changes:

- **Think in one-week chunks.** Don't try to figure out the rest of your life when you're feeling low. Just decide what you'd like to accomplish in the next week and write it down. Get specific, and plan which day you'd like to do each activity. Regular contact with your mental health team is a given, but also be sure to schedule physical activity, time with people you like, some meaningful work (whether paid or voluntary), and in pleasant activities. Plan each day in the context of your desired week.

- **Set moderate goals.** By moderate, I mean be aware of your current reality and degree of lethargy, and then plan activities that take you slightly outside your comfort zone every day. If you're catatonic and immobilized in bed, just putting on your shoes and spending a few minutes outdoors is a victory.
- **Celebrate progress.** When you achieve what you planned, acknowledge and celebrate your progress. Ask loved ones to help with this. Also be gentle with yourself. If you don't do what you planned, don't beat yourself up. Maybe it wasn't possible that day. Resolve to give it your best shot the next day.
- **Schedule some pleasant activities.** If you feel that you don't know how to have fun, try to recall activities that you've enjoyed in the past. If you can't remember any, ask a friend or loved one for help with this. Also be open to new experiences, which can help you get outside your head. Here are some ideas for new or pleasant activities:
    - Take photographs
    - Take a bath
    - Make a cake
    - Play with a pet
    - Listen to music
    - Learn something new
    - Go on a picnic
    - Paddle a kayak or canoe
    - Go to the beach
    - Ride a ferry

- Visit a museum
- Watch the stars
- Draw
- Go on a beautiful hike
- Go for a walk
- Read an inspiring book
- Listen to a relaxation CD
- Have coffee with a friend
- Volunteer your time
- Watch live music
- Cook something
- Go to the library and explore
- Go to the theater
- Putter in the garden
- Play a musical instrument
- Get a massage
- Watch a good movie
- Go to the gym
- Ride a bike
- Watch a comedian
- Go on a scenic drive
- Learn a craft

One final thought: When people are depressed, they tend to be preoccupied with their difficulties. It's easy to get caught up in your feelings, especially when you're struggling, but don't forget to ask your loved ones about their lives and how they're feeling. When I was down, I had no idea how much my illness was impacting those around me. If I had checked in with them and understood this, it might have helped me take a wider perspective. It's healthy and beneficial to sometimes focus on others and ask them, "Are you okay?"

This is the end of the book, but not the end of your journey. As you travel forward, I hope this book has helped you feel less alone and more hopeful. If it were possible I would look you in the eye and say, "Depression does pass. At one point I didn't believe it was possible, but now I know it is."

On reviewing the interviews in this book, I want to say that each person I interviewed has gone on to lead a very meaningful life, and I think a quality they all share is feeling enormously fulfilled by telling their story of hope and advocating to end the stigma associated with depression and other mental illnesses. I believe this kind of work is key to long-term, sustainable recovery.

Please take hope—and take action. May the best in life and love and happiness be ahead of you.

AFTERWORD

by Allen Doederlein

Graeme Cowan's *Back from the Brink* is an important contribution to the literature about depression and bipolar disorder, and we at the Depression and Bipolar Support Alliance (DBSA) are thrilled to be aligned with the book, and with Graeme. Graeme's story, along with the narratives of the eight "fellow travelers" he interviews in this extraordinary book, illustrates one of DBSA's core values: that the accomplishments of people with mood disorders are numerous, inspiring, and deserving of celebration.

All too often, we hear only part of the story about depression and bipolar disorder: what's wrong, what's bad, and what can be done to reduce symptoms. We talk about surviving. And we don't tell the full, inspiring story of wellness: what strengths and resiliencies we have that help to fix what's wrong, what good things we learn from our bad experiences with mood issues, and how people can and do become truly well. We need to start talking about thriving.

Shifting the conversation about mood disorders from surviving to thriving doesn't mean that we ignore or underestimate the life-threatening struggles that come with these serious diagnoses. Nor do Graeme, his peers whose stories are chronicled in this book, or we at DBSA suggest that to make it "back from the brink" is easy. It's a lot of work, work that usually takes place simultaneously on many different fronts. Various forms of therapy, medication, peer support, exercise, meditation and mindfulness, and meaningful employment or work in the community: all of these treatments and strategies are combined, recombined, and refined by those interviewed in *Back from the Brink.* Wellness and thriving are not finite destinations; rather, they are journeys.

Another important theme in many of the stories shared in *Back from the Brink* is that to give back to others is uniquely beneficial in attaining and maintaining a thriving existence. Of course that's fundamental to DBSA, which has three hundred chapters across the United States that create forums for such advocacy and sharing. I hope that readers of this book will be inspired, as they so often are by DBSA, not only to seek thriving lives, but also to give back to their peers by sharing their personal experiences, becoming advocates, and acting as living examples of the full story of thriving.

We at DBSA applaud Graeme and his peers, who have shared their stories of thriving in this special book. Together, people like Graeme Cowan, books like *Back from the Brink*, and organizations like the Depression and Bipolar Support Alliance are creating a world where we don't just talk about eradicating illness; we also talk about creating, maintaining, and celebrating wellness.

—Allen Doederlein
President, Depression and Bipolar Support Alliance

RESOURCES

CRISIS HOTLINE

National Suicide Prevention Lifeline:
http://http://www.suicidepreventionlifeline.org

This organization offers a 24/7 crisis helpline: 1-800-273-TALK (8255).

DEPRESSION AND BIPOLAR DISORDER INFORMATION AND SUPPORT GROUPS

Black Dog Institute: http://http://www.blackdoginstitute.org.au

This Australian site has a fantastic multimedia education program about depression and bipolar disorder and effective treatments. The site also offers self-tests and downloadable brochures.

Depression and Bipolar Support Alliance (DBSA):
http://http://www.dbsalliance.org

DBSA's website offers information on depression and bipolar disorder, resources for finding services, peer support programs, and both online and local support groups. I highly recommend the Wellness Toolbox.

National Institute of Mental Health: http://www.nimh.nih.gov

This government site provides a wide range of information related to depression and bipolar disorder, including downloadable brochures and books and a search engine for finding local resources.

Substance Abuse and Mental Health Services Administration: http://www.samhsa.gov

This site has a Treatment Locator that helps identify mental health services near you, and helpful publications that you can purchase online. It also has a 24/7 help treatment line: 1-800-662-4357.

EMOTIONAL SUPPORT

Compeer: http://www.compeer.org

An organization that provides volunteer friends to people isolated by a mental illness. It operates in several locations across the United States.

Depression Recovery Groups at Support Groups Central: http://www.supportgroupscentral.com/depression

In addition to online support groups, including groups for teens and college students, this organization offers one-on-one, online depression recovery coaching.

Meetup: http://www.meetup.com

This site allows you to join or form local groups for walking and pursuing shared interests.

National Alliance on Mental Illness (NAMI): http://www.nami.org

NAMI offers peer support and online discussion groups, as well as information, and also has local chapters and support groups.

APPS AND ONLINE PROGRAMS

Beacon: http://www.beacon.anu.edu.au

This website reviews and rates Internet programs, apps, and online support groups for a variety of health and mental health concerns.

Depression CBT Self-Help Guide (Android app, available through Google Play)

This app uses the principles of cognitive behavioral therapy to help people learn to control the stress that contributes to depression.

MoodGYM: http://www.moodgym.anu.edu.au

This free, online, cognitive behavioral therapy program, developed by the Australian National University, is designed to help young people prevent or cope with depression. It has been utilized in over 130 countries, and peer-reviewed studies have shown that it has excellent results.

Optimism Apps: http://www.findingoptimism.com

This company offers apps designed to help people increase their understanding of the factors that affect their mental health. The apps detect patterns in people's health, and offer strategies to proactively manage depression, bipolar disorder, and other mental health conditions.

REVITALIZING WORK

Good2Gether: http://www.good2gether.com

Good2Gether is a website and smartphone app to connect businesses that do good, consumers who care, and the local causes they both support.

Idealist: http://www.idealist.org

Idealist connects people with organizations for the greater good in the United States and around the world.

LinkedIn Back from the Brink Work Support Group: http://www.linkedin.com/groups/Back-From-Brink-Work-Support-4854845

This LinkedIn group is dedicated to helping people with depression and bipolar disorder find fulfilling work.

US Office of Disability Employment Policy Return to Work Toolkit: http://www.dol.gov/odep/return-to-work

This resource, provided by the US Department of Labor, is helpful for both employees and employers.

VolunteerMatch: http://www.volunteermatch.org

This website helps connect volunteers with opportunities to serve.

EXERCISE

MapMyWalk App: http://www.mapmywalk.com

This fitness-tracking app allows you to track your walks and other activities using a smartphone's GPS function. It was voted best app in the 2012 Walking Readers' Choice Awards at walking .about.com.

SparkPeople: http://www.sparkpeople.com

This website offers many fitness resources and helps connect people with the common goal of exercising more and getting healthier.

MEDITATION

Brahma Kumaris World Spiritual University: http://www.brahmakumaris.org

This organization offers meditation classes in over 110 countries.

RESOURCES FOR CAREGIVERS

Bipolar Caregivers: http://www.bipolarcaregivers.org

This site offers practical advice on caring for someone with bipolar disorder, including a downloadable e-book.

Caregiver.com: http://www.caregiver.com

This organization—which is aimed at all caregivers, not just those caring for someone with mental health issues—also publishes a magazine.

Families for Depression Awareness: http://www.familyaware.org

This organization helps families recognize and cope with a loved one's depression and offers information on how to promote recovery. They offer particularly good depression and bipolar disorder wellness guides for parents, teens, and schools.

Bipolar Significant Others (BPSO): http://www.bpso.org

Caregivers will find good practical advice and online support and discussion groups at this website.

GRAEME COWAN ONLINE

Website: http://www.iambackfromthebrink.com

I offer a variety of resources on my website, where you can also read my blog, listen to podcasts, view videos, and more. At www.iambackfromthebrink.com/30DayChallenge, you can register for a thirty-day program to boost your mood; each day of the challenge, you'll receive an e-mail with practical suggestions that can help you out of the black hole.

YouTube channel: http://www.youtube.com/Strive2ThriveTV

My YouTube channel provides videos with further insights into helpful strategies for recovering from depression or bipolar disorder.

Facebook: http://www.facebook.com/BackfromtheBrink

REFERENCES

Buckingham, M. 2011. *StandOut: The Groundbreaking New Strengths Assessment from the Leader of the Strengths Revolution.* Nashville, TN: Thomas Nelson.

Buettner, D. 2005. "New Wrinkles on Aging." *National Geographic*, November, 2–19.

Campbell, A. 2007. *The Blair Years: The Alastair Campbell Diaries.* New York: Alfred A. Knopf.

Clarke, A. E., E. Diener, Y. Georgellis, and R. E. Lucas. 2008. "Lags and Leads in Life Satisfaction: A Test of Baseline Hypothesis." *Economic Journal* 118 (529): 222–243.

Einstein, A. 2011. *The Ultimate Quotable Einstein.* Princeton, NJ: Princeton University Press.

Freedman, D. 2010. *Wrong: Why Experts Keep Failing Us—And How to Know When Not to Trust Them.* New York: Little, Brown.

Freeman, M. P. 2010. "Nutrition and Psychiatry." *American Journal of Psychiatry* 167 (3): 244–247.

Ghaemi, N. 2012. *A First-Rate Madness: Uncovering the Links Between Leadership and Mental Illness.* New York: Penguin.

Glowinski, A., P. Madden, K. Bucholz, M. Lynskey, and A. Heath. 2003. "Genetic Epidemiology of Self-Reported Lifetime DSM-IV Major Depressive Disorder in a Population-Based Twin Sample of Female Adolescents." *Journal of Child Psychology and Psychiatry* 44 (7): 988–996.

Goddard, T. 2009. *Trisha: A Life Less Ordinary.* London: John Blake Publishing.

Hibbeln, J. R. 1998. "Fish Consumption and Major Depression." *Lancet* 351 (9110): 1213.

Inman, L. 2008. *Running Uphill: A Memoir of Surviving Depressive Illness.* Jacksonville Beach, FL: High-Pitched Hum Publishing.

Ioannidis, J. P. A. 2005. "Why Most Published Research Findings Are False." *PLOS Medicine* 28 (8): e124.

Jacka, F., P. J. Kremer, M. Berk, A. M. de Silva-Sanigorski, M. Moodie, E. R. Leslie, J. A. Pasco, and B. A. Swinburn. 2011. "A Prospective Study of Diet Quality and Mental Health in Adolescents." *PLOS One* 6 (3): e24805.

Krucoff, C., and M. Krucoff. 2000. "Peak Performance." *American Fitness* 19 (6): 32–36.

Loehr, J., and T. Schwartz. 2005. *The Power of Full Engagement: Managing Energy, Not Time, Is the Key to High Performance and Personal Renewal.* New York: Free Press.

Lyubomirsky, S. 2008. *The How of Happiness: A New Approach to Getting the Life You Want.* New York: Penguin.

Martin, L. R., S. L. Williams, K. B. Haskard, and M. R. DiMatteo. 2005. "The Challenge of Patient Adherence." *Therapeutics and Clinical Risk Management* 1 (3): 189–199.

Mayo Clinic. 2008. "Moderate Exercise." *Mayo Clinic Health Letter* 26 (1): 1–3.

Morgan, A. L., D. A. Tobar, and L. Snyder. 2010. "Walking Toward a New Me: The Impact of Prescribed Walking 10,000 Steps/Day on Physical and Psychological Well-Being." *Journal of Physical Activity and Health* 7 (3): 299–307.

Parker, G. (ed). 2012. *Bipolar II Disorder: Modelling, Measuring, and Managing.* Cambridge, UK: Cambridge University Press.

Parker, G., and D. Hadzi-Pavlovic. 1996. *Melancholia: A Disorder of Movement and Mood.* Cambridge, UK: Cambridge University Press.

Parker, G., D. Hadzi-Pavlovic, I. Hickie, P. Mitchell, K. Wilhelm, H. Brodaty, P. Boyce, K. Eyers, and F. Pedic. 1991. "Psychotic Depression: A Review and Clinical Experience." *Australian and New Zealand Journal of Psychiatry* 25 (2): 169–180.

Parker, G., and V. Manicavasagar. 2005. *Modelling and Managing the Depressive Disorders.* Cambridge, UK: Cambridge University Press.

Parker, G., S. McCraw, D. Hadzi-Pavlovic, M. Hong, and M. Barrett. 2012. "Bipolar Depression: Prototypically Melancholic in Its Clinical Features." *Journal of Affective Disorders* 147 (1–3): 331–337.

Rath, T. 2007. *StrengthsFinder 2.0.* New York: Gallup Press.

Rath, T., and J. K. Harter. 2010. *Wellbeing: The Five Essential Elements.* New York: Gallup Press.

Richey, C. 2010. *Acing Depression: A Tennis Champion's Toughest Match.* New York: New Chapter Press.

Seligman, M. 2002. *Authentic Happiness: Using the New Positive Psychology to Realize Your Potential for Lasting Fulfillment.* New York: Free Press.

Seligman, M. 2011. *Flourish: A Visionary New Understanding of Happiness and Well-Being.* New York: Free Press.

Teasdale, J. D., Z. V. Segal, J. M. G. Williams, V. A. Ridgeway, J. M. Soulsby, and M. A. Lau. 2000. "Prevention of Relapse/Recurrence in Major Depression by Mindfulness-Based Cognitive Therapy." *Journal of Consulting and Clinical Psychology* 68 (4): 615–623.

Ware, B. 2012. *The Top Five Regrets of the Dying: A Life Transformed by the Dearly Departing.* Carlsbad, CA: Hay House.

World Health Organization. 2001. *The World Health Report 2001. Mental Health: New Understanding, New Hope.* Geneva, Switzerland: World Health Organization.

Zettle, R. D., and J. Rains. 1989. "Group Cognitive and Contextual Therapies in Treatment of Depression." *Journal of Clinical Psychology* 45 (3): 438–445.

Graeme Cowan lived through a five-year episode of depression that his psychiatrist described as the worst he had ever treated. This fueled his desire to prevent others from going through the same thing. Through this horrific experience, and his own extensive research, he has guided, taught, and inspired countless people through his books, keynote presentations, and media appearances.

Foreword writer **Glenn Close** is an Emmy, Golden Globe, and Tony Award-winning actress who made her feature film debut in *The World According to Garp*. Her performance earned Close her first Academy Award nomination. She was subsequently Oscar-nominated for her performances in *The Big Chill, The Natural, Fatal Attraction, Dangerous Liaisons*, and most recently, *Albert Nobbs*, which she also cowrote and produced. Among her television credits is the highly-acclaimed TV legal drama, *Damages*, for which she has won two Emmy Awards and a Golden Globe as Best Actress.

In 2009, Close participated in the launch of Bring Change 2 Mind, a non-profit organization working to end the stigma, misunderstanding, and discrimination surrounding mental illness. The idea for this movement evolved out of her first-hand observation of battles with mental illness within her family. Her sister, Jessie, lives with bipolar disorder and Jessie's son, Calen, is living with schizoaffective disorder.

Afterword writer **Allen Doederlein** is president of the Depression and Bipolar Support Alliance (DBSA), the nation's largest consumer-led mental health organization focusing on mood disorders, and a proud member of the advocacy committee of the International Society of Bipolar Disorders.

FROM OUR PUBLISHER—

As the publisher at New Harbinger and a clinical psychologist since 1978, I know that emotional problems are best helped with evidence-based therapies. These are the treatments derived from scientific research (randomized controlled trials) that show what works. Whether these treatments are delivered by trained clinicians or found in a self-help book, they are designed to provide you with proven strategies to overcome your problem.

Therapies that aren't evidence-based—whether offered by clinicians or in books—are much less likely to help. In fact, therapies that aren't guided by science may not help you at all. That's why this New Harbinger book is based on scientific evidence that the treatment can relieve emotional pain.

This is important: if this book isn't enough, and you need the help of a skilled therapist, use the following resources to find a clinician trained in the evidence-based protocols appropriate for your problem. And if you need more support—a community that understands what you're going through and can show you ways to cope—resources for that are provided below, as well.

Real help is available for the problems you have been struggling with. The skills you can learn from evidence-based therapies will change your life.

Matthew McKay, PhD
Publisher, New Harbinger Publications

If you need a therapist, the following organization can help you find a therapist trained in cognitive behavioral therapy (CBT).

The Association for Behavioral & Cognitive Therapies (ABCT) Find-a-Therapist service offers a list of therapists schooled in CBT techniques. Therapists listed are licensed professionals who have met the membership requirements of ABCT and who have chosen to appear in the directory.

Please visit www.abct.org and click on *Find a Therapist*.

For additional support for patients, family, and friends, please contact the following:

Anxiety and Depression Association of America (ADAA)
Visit www.adaa.org

Depression and Bipolar Support Alliance (DBSA)
visit www.dbsalliance.org

National Alliance on Mental Illness (NAMI)
please visit www.nami.org